Inside Training & Development:
Creating Effective Programs

Inside Training & Development: Creating Effective Programs

Susan Warshauer

University Associates, Inc.
8517 Production Avenue
San Diego, California 92121

ISBN: 0-88390-218-4
Library of Congress Catalog Card Number: 88-6921
Printed in the United States of America

Library of Congress Cataloging-in-Publication Data

Warshauer, Susan.
    Inside training and development: creating effective programs/
Susan Warshauer.
       p.   cm.
    Bibliography: p.
    ISBN 0-88390-218-4
    1. Employees, Training of. 2. Career development. I. Title.
HF5549.5.T7W375   1988
658.3′ 12404—dc19
                                       88-6921
                                          CIP

The author and the publisher gratefully acknowledge permission to reprint quotes from the following sources:

1. American Society for Training and Development, for quotes from:

    Christensen, D.R., & Kinlaw, D.C. (1984). Management training: Managers can do it all—or almost all. *Training and Development Journal, 38,* 87-89. Quotes from Christensen and Kinlaw appear on pages 110, 111, and 113 of this book.

    Faris, J.P. (1984). How to use films in training. *Training and Development Journal, 38,* 108-110. Quotes from Faris appear on pages 75 and 77 of this book.

    Gall, A.L. (Ed.). (1986). Four by four: How do you develop a training program on an unfamiliar topic? *Training and Development Journal, 40,* 22-25. Quotes from Gall appear on pages 44, 48, and 54 of this book.

    Hutcheson, P., & Otte, F. (1981). *Careers in training and development.* Alexandria, VA: American Society for Training and Development. Quotes from Hutcheson and Otte appear on pages 152 and 153 of this book.

    Trost, A. (1985). They may love it but will they use it? *Training and Development Journal, 39,* 78-81. Quotes from Trost appear on pages 90 and 94 of this book.

    Wlodkowski, R. (1985). Stimulation. *Training and Development Journal, 39,* 38-43. Quotes from Wlodkowski appear on pages 57 and 66 of this book.

2. Harper & Row, for quotes from:

    Michalak, D.F., & Yager, E.G. (1979). *Making the training process work.* New York: Harper & Row. Quotes from Michalak and Yager appear on pages 18, 89, 90, and 91 of this book.

Cover Design & Production Art by Janet Colby

In Appreciation

No one writes a book alone. This book would not be in your hands without the support, contributions, encouragement, critiques, and good-natured ribbing of many people. I am indeed fortunate that many individuals volunteered to help—some freely and some under a little duress—and thus greatly enriched the process for me.

I especially want to acknowledge those who were central to my efforts:

I dedicate this volume to Paul Korn. I never would have accepted the challenge of writing it without his cooperation, support, and love. It is astounding that a man who appropriately and routinely sports a T-shirt saying "Lost in Space" provided my anchor to reality during this process!

To Dick Roe, who provided me with the opportunity to write this book, the encouragement to continue, and the impetus to finish.

To my dear friends, family, colleagues, and neighbors, who provided ideas, suggestions, criticism, and continual encouragement.

To my teachers, from whom I learned to be creative and to take thoughtful risks.

To those who helped to get all of these words on paper, in order, and looking good. My special appreciation goes to Rosanne Shapiro.

And, last but not least, to my sons, Jonathan and Nicholas, for letting me write this book and still loving me.

Thank you all.

Preface

Early in a workshop or other training program the approach of most trainers is to spend some time clarifying goals and providing participants with an overview of program content and structure. Participants seem to find it easier to trust the process of a workshop and the credibility of a trainer if they know what garden paths they are being led down and why. Similarly, it might be helpful to the reader to know why this book was written, who it was written for, and what its primary focus is.

The field of training and development has grown enormously over the past few years. It has been estimated that in the United States organizations spend approximately $30 billion a year on formal employee-training programs. In addition, the sum of approximately $180 billion a year is spent on informal training and coaching (Carnevale, 1986).

The impetus to begin training and development in an organization or to hire external professionals for this purpose often comes from management's sincere belief that training activities are an important addition to the benefits and services already offered to employees, that they are a worthwhile investment, and that they will help employees to develop and to fulfill their potential. Furthermore, management hopes that training and development will increase personal and job satisfaction, increase motivation and productivity, and decrease turnover.

There are other reasons for the increased visibility and credibility of training and development. Some companies have jumped on the bandwagon because their competitors have done likewise; others have launched efforts in response to perceived threats of unionization. In some cases employees themselves provide the impetus for training efforts. Today's employees tend to be more assertive and sophisticated about their own development than they were years ago; also, they are more knowledgeable about the kinds of training opportunities offered in other organizations and are concerned with developing their careers rather than just doing their jobs.

With the growth in the field of training has come an increase in the number of small training functions, both independent and within organizations. Due to economic concerns, organizations that want internal training functions often start small. Many companies that are concerned with cost effectiveness and justification of their investments adopt the strategy of maintaining small training staffs—sometimes downsizing existing staffs—and hiring consultants to fill the gaps, thereby limiting employee-benefit costs; others have no training staffs and instead contract with small, independent training organizations, thereby eliminating the problem of employee-benefit costs.

It is not uncommon for trainers to work alone or with just a few colleagues, whether they are independent or employees of larger organizations. Sometimes organizations assign personnel to the training function on a part-time basis only. Individuals who have shown an interest in training or have some limited teaching experience are sometimes drafted to "see what can be done." On some occasions an individual in an organization will become enthusiastic about conducting training after having been a participant in a program and will sell the idea to the organization or to a senior manager.

Regardless of the way in which people become members of small training functions, they soon discover that training is a field in which experience matters a great deal. Experience provides exposure to techniques, ideas, and styles; it also builds self-confidence and effectiveness. This book is intended to be a resource for those working in the field, especially members of small, new, or recently downsized training functions. It also can be used as a catalyst for review and discussion among trainers in evaluating and revamping their efforts. Because so many trainers work alone or in small training functions, it can be a revitalizing and rejuvenating experience to learn how others perform their roles. Therefore, I hope that this book will be used as a stimulus for self-reflection. Individuals who are interested in entering the field of training and development may also find this book useful as a source of information about the skills needed and the major issues and concerns involved in training.

The major thrust of this book is to increase the reader's awareness of the political implications of various choices that are made in connection with training. One chapter is devoted to the politics of managing a training function; in addition, the political implications of different options are examined throughout the book. The reader is encouraged to reflect on the unique political implications of the environment(s) in which he or she works.

This book concerns the process of developing a *viable* training function; ideals are not dealt with. It emphasizes the importance of knowing as much as possible about the dynamics of an organization—whether the organization is the trainer's employer or client—and the major players in it, understanding the true meaning of training and development in that organization, and making informed decisions based on thoughtful strategies that will increase the likelihood of achieving the organization's mission and goals regarding training. In connection with increasing viability, the issue of developing widespread support within an organization is also emphasized in several chapters.

I have tried to make the format of this book consistent with my values and beliefs about how people learn best. I have applied the same guiding principles that I use in designing training programs. In addition, I have tried to balance theory and practice; discussions of concepts are combined with many concrete examples as well as questions regarding applications. I want to provoke readers to think about the settings in which they work and to question critically the application of different suggestions and concepts. I have tried to provide enough examples from different kinds of organizations to increase relevance. Although the issues raised in the cases are real, the details have been changed to disguise their origins.

The tone of this book is intentionally conversational. Write in this book, adapt it, use ideas from it—make it your volume, too. I hope that it will become a colleague of sorts—that you will pick it up often to find ideas, to clarify your thoughts and perceptions, and to lend it to others for the purpose of generating discussions.

Susan Warshauer
Cambridge, Massachusetts

January, 1988

Contents

1

Developing Political Awareness

Politics exists in all organizations. Individuals who recognize the political component of their jobs are more likely to be successful and effective in achieving their goals. It is naive and often self-defeating to believe that ideas are judged solely on their merits. The relationship of the idea generator to decision makers in the organization, the timing and method of an idea's presentation, and the interpersonal communication skills of those involved all contribute to the likelihood that an idea will be adopted. Individuals who realize the complexity of organizational dynamics and the interrelationships of the players are able to develop strategies about ways to increase their success in accomplishing their goals.

Political awareness includes an acknowledgment that many forces in an organization determine the directions that are chosen. Political awareness means applying knowledge of the way in which things get done, of who has decision-making power on an issue, of supports and resistances that might exist, and of how to pave the way for receptivity to an idea. It also implies advance planning and strategy development. Contrary to popular opinion, political savvy is often associated with ethical and trustworthy behavior. Unfortunately, some people still see the use of political awareness as a manipulative, unattractive method of behaving. However, it is irresponsible *not* to apply knowledge of how to get through the politics of an organization and accomplish a goal. Developing a strategy and doing advance planning to launch an idea or program can save a company money and time. Useful ideas can be more efficiently and effectively implemented if the organization is ripe and receptive.

This chapter is about developing political awareness. It includes discussions of the areas of responsibility and types of interactions to consider to increase the likelihood of success as a training and development professional and as an organizational team member. Many decisions and courses of action of trainers have far-reaching implications for organizations. This chapter attempts to heighten awareness of the sometimes unintended and seemingly peripheral outcomes and influences that training interventions can cause. It also attempts to remind trainers to pause and think through strategies of action carefully before launching new ideas or programs. Thoughtful political behavior can support a training function and can increase its visibility, credibility, and clout. In addition, this chapter includes an exploration of the issues involved in developing an operational definition of training in an organization; the importance of being consistent and conducting ongoing diagnoses of the trends, influences, and power dynamics in an organization; the concept of where training is politically situated in an organization; and strategic thinking as a mode of operation.

DEFINITION OF TRAINING AND DEVELOPMENT IN AN ORGANIZATION

History

A peek into the history of training and development in an organization can do a lot to clarify how the function is perceived and received in that organization. Knowledge of the impetus to create a training function can shed light on the supports and resistances that exist. Talking to old-timers and home-grown senior managers can provide interesting anecdotes that give a context and a framework for increasing the future success of training efforts. Finding out about the intended consequences of the original efforts to begin training and development programs, as well as the trends and influences that strengthened or changed those first notions, can help significantly in planning programs that have an increased likelihood of success.

> ### Example: Using knowledge of the history of training in an organization to influence future directions.
>
> *Tom was hired by a hospital as the director of training. As he interviewed managers at various levels and in various areas, he discovered that his predecessor had been influenced to leave by Mildred, the new vice president for human resources.*

Furthermore, Tom learned that the hospital had grown enormously in the past two years and that most of the senior administrative positions had turned over. Before Mildred was hired, the training function had been under the supervision of the senior vice president, who had mandated its creation. When he retired, a new position—vice president for human resources—was created, and Mildred was hired to fill it. Mildred held an M.B.A. from a prestigious school.

Unlike the previous management, Mildred was interested in whether training was increasing effectiveness, cutting costs, and improving morale. She did not support programs oriented toward personal development; she wanted short, focused, relevant training that taught skills and built self-confidence. Tom's predecessor had been active in the Sixties' style of human relations training. Tom understood the handwriting on the wall and developed a series of job-related training modules for different groups of employees. He cultivated hospital-wide visibility and credibility with these initial offerings. As time passed, he was able to convince Mildred of the need to offer programs geared toward personal development. The payoffs of such programs would be increased morale and job satisfaction.

Defining the Training Function

Within the context of the history of training and development in an organization, trainers and training directors need to be clear about their own definitions of the function. They need to think through what they see as their charge and their mission. Personal definitions of training determine what trainers will or will not agree to do in an organization, help them to stay focused, and facilitate choices that contribute to their goals and mission. By publicizing a definition of its mission, a training function can help educate managers and employees about what it can and cannot do.

Determining a definition of training in an organization is not a solitary activity. To be most effective and realistic, the definition—including the mission and charge of the training function—is developed through reiterations with management and members of the community. It is not a static definition, but is reviewed and fine-tuned regularly. It contains statements that reflect the role of training in an organization, anchored in the human resource philosophy of that organization, and should not be a restrictive mandate that curtails creativity.

Influencing the Meaning of Training and Development

There are many roles that trainers can play. As trainers develop credibility and visibility in an organization, the notion of training and development often is expanded beyond training events.

As internal consultants in an organization, trainers can intervene more easily if programs are not the immediate answer to a problem. For example, while working with managers to investigate and determine obstacles to better performance and increased job satisfaction in a department, trainers can recommend a variety of solutions, including job restructuring, performance coaching, team building, or training programs. The transition from trainer to organization development consultant often begins this way.

As resident experts on resources within an organization or in the outside community, trainers might be asked to provide the names of consultants for technical training programs, to help managers in interviewing and selecting consultants, or to recommend executive development programs for senior managers.

Trainers can be involved in efforts to provide career-development activities other than training programs. They can function as chairpersons or resources to advisory groups developing career paths, job-rotation programs, individualized development plans, or internships.

Efforts to support change in an organization, or to increase job satisfaction through policies like flex-time or child-care programs, can cause disruption. A trainer's perspective can help to ease transition and to increase acceptance by members of an organization.

Managers, supervisors, and other workshop participants often use trainers as informal confidants or counselors. By intervening in conflicts between supervisors and employees, trainers can provide career counseling, be a sounding board for confused employees, or make referrals for individuals with personal problems.

As role definitions of training and development professionals in an organization broaden, the influence of those professionals increases and the range of skills required grows. Sometimes individuals get in over their heads by involvement with projects that go beyond the scope of their skills. By hiring consultants, trainers can avert disaster and still be challenged and stretched in their jobs. While primary responsibility can then be placed with more skilled professionals, trainers can remain involved and increase their knowledge.

The appropriateness of training as an organizational response should be questioned consciously. Trainers need to be very careful not to raise unrealistic expectations about what training can or cannot do.

Working within departments can sometimes be more effective than offering generic organization-wide training programs. Tailored programs can address relevant problems in local jargon and can increase credibility. A chance to provide a program tailored to a specific organization can sometimes yield the additional opportunity of using skills as an internal consultant to look at a department as a whole and to effect change.

Example: Using a tailored training program as a kickoff to system-wide change.

Edna, a training director, was asked to conduct workshops for managers on running better meetings in a department that functioned largely on the basis of committees. She met with a senior manager, and together they decided not only to sponsor the workshops on running meetings but also to organize a subsequent series of workshops for all employees on being more effective participants in meetings.

After finishing the workshops, Edna met with senior management and summarized the major complaints and suggestions she had heard about the way in which committees worked in the department. She proposed a number of changes concerning the policies and procedures used in establishing, running, and following up committee work. The effect of the system-wide involvement was to create an environment with heightened awareness, concern, and motivation to improve the functioning and productivity of the committee structure. In effect, a critical mass of trained personnel was established. Employees felt that management had listened to and acted on their concerns and suggestions.

Novel opportunities to help can occur when trainers remain flexible and open. For instance, trainers can operate as resources to task groups even if the content of the meetings is out of their realm of expertise. As group-process consultants and educated observers of dynamics, they can help groups to make decisions, reach compromises, and function more effectively. Since time is limited, trainers must make conscious choices of those involvements that make the most sense.

Example: Using a trainer's skills creatively.

The personnel office of a savings and loan association wanted to find out why employee turnover was so high among branch tellers. Senior management decided to conduct exit interviews of all employees who had left the bank during the previous year. The training department was contacted to help the personnel office to develop a format for the interviews that would allow for consistency of data collection and ease of analysis. As a result of this work and of the relationships and credibility that were established, the training department proposed and implemented a series of programs for branch tellers.

The nature of trainers' work gives them the unique mandate to gather groups of people in the work place. Workshops can provide opportunities for employees at all levels to meet colleagues from different parts of an organization. When program participants represent a cross section of the organization, it is common to hear, "Oh, you're Jane in accounting. I've talked to you a zillion times!" or "I've heard your name and I've always wondered who you were." The networking aspect of training programs can open and improve communication.

Bringing people together is a powerful act and can have many planned and unplanned repercussions. These opportunities can be used to further the organizational mission, goals, and objectives. Because participants go back to their own units, they can effect change. The act of gathering people together and providing focused forums can influence the nature of change and the motivation and confidence of the emissaries of change. Programs need to accomplish some of what they are being directly requested to do, but there are ways to cover required content and still support and move toward accomplishing organizational goals.

CONSISTENCY

In successful training efforts, consistency is a central value and a key strategy. Thoughtful consistency should exist between mission and behavior in an organization. The theories and concepts of effective organizational behavior that are espoused should be applied. Trainers must be conscientious about asking others to do only what they themselves are willing to do.

Consistency and rigidity are not the same. Trainers need to remain flexible and open in order to analyze new situations and develop realistic strategies, but key values behind those strategies must be addressed consistently.

Role Modeling

Trainers and training functions can gain credibility by modeling effective behavior.

> **Example: Using role modeling to influence supervisory behavior.**
>
> *One session of a program designed for supervisors focused on career development and the supervisory role. Much of the session was devoted to what supervisors could do to provide for and support the development of their staff members. The trainer in the workshop emphasized the importance of supervisory support in encouraging transfer of learning from training programs to the work place. He suggested several techniques that supervisors could use to help in the process of transfering learning: discussing expectations and goals before a workshop, providing opportunities for employees to use new skills on the job, and discussing employees' efforts to apply the skills.*
>
> *After the supervisory program was over, the trainer used some of the suggested techniques to encourage transfer of learning for the supervisors themselves. He sent follow-up readings and invited specific supervisors to hear speakers on relevant subjects. Several months after the program ended, he sent follow-up questionnaires asking the supervisors to look at their original goals for the program and report their efforts to apply the concepts and techniques that had been taught.*
>
> *By attempting to support the supervisors' learnings, the trainer also modeled the behavior that he was asking them to try with their own employees.*

A conscientious trainer who tries to apply the concepts espoused has the best chance of building a solid reputation and a keen understanding of the difficulties of applying theories.

Supporting Organizational Goals and Values

It is critical for trainers to stay in touch with both the organizational mission and the goals of senior management. In order to determine how the training function can help the organization to achieve its goals, trainers need to be clear about what those goals are.

Training activities, by their nature, promote change. Trainers need to promote change in directions that support the missions, goals, and objectives of the organizations themselves. Understanding the values and goals of an organization allows for their integration into programs.

Example: Using training to support organizational values.

Knowing that the company she worked for was very committed to providing a work environment free of discriminatory behavior, a training director was frustrated in her attempts to get supervisors to attend programs on racism and sexism. At a staff meeting, the trainers developed a strategy to integrate the organizational value of creating a nondiscriminatory work setting into many existing training programs. They incorporated cases involving subtle and overt examples of racist and sexist behavior into many supervisory courses and courses on nonsupervisory communication. For instance, supervisors discussed how they would deal with situations in which employees were heard telling racist jokes.

Because the cases were integrated into many programs, more people were exposed to the issues and to the organizational values regarding discriminatory behavior. Individuals who would not attend a session focused on racism or sexism developed an increased awareness of these issues and the organization's stance.

Relevant Training

Transfer of learning from workshops to job settings increases if the concepts and applications taught are ones that can easily be used. For example, supervisors who are taught about participative management and are encouraged to try such techniques will question the usefulness of their training if they are sent back to managers who are not interested in increasing participation. Learning about the participant's home organization makes it easier to provide more relevant training. Giving participants glimpses into how concepts relate to the organization as a whole can support their efforts to apply these concepts on the job.

It is important to help employees to learn concepts and skills, but it is just as important to equip and empower them to apply those concepts and skills.

DIAGNOSIS

The best trainers learn about the business of their companies by conducting excellent and continuing diagnoses of the structure, culture, myths, critical issues, processes of decision making, and power figures. Desatnick (1984, p. 42) reports that in a study of twenty-six companies "the successful human resource professional undertook their mission with a clear understanding of the business, its needs and priorities."

Learning about an organization and its history clarifies the identity of the players, the significant organizational issues, and the changes in priorities and needs. This kind of knowledge increases effectiveness and credibility. It helps trainers to form favorable alliances, recognize opportunities, and make appropriate choices. Studying existing documents—including strategic plans, policy manuals, transcripts of speeches, and reports—can lead to an understanding of organizational issues.

Organizational Structure

The way in which the training function fits into the organizational structure has implications for the viability and impact of that function. For example, in some organizations the training function reports directly to a vice president or senior manager; in other companies training is under the sponsorship of the director of personnel. Training professionals cannot usually alter the established structure, although sometimes they can influence decision making during reorganization efforts. It can be important to understand the history, rationale, and implications of the placement of training and development within the organizational structure and to recognize supports and obstacles.

Benefits of Confidants

There are times in organizational life when it is extremely useful to have access to knowledgeable and trustworthy counsel. Sometimes another perspective can clear muddy waters, build beneficial bridges, or provide a missing piece of information to aid understanding. The availability of a confidant is especially important for those working in single-person training functions.

In the most fortunate circumstances, an employee can trust his or her immediate supervisor as a confidant—someone who has the employee's best interests at heart, who does not routinely operate from hidden agendas, and who encourages the employee's growth and development. If an immediate supervisor cannot provide this service, it can be quite useful to seek out such a person elsewhere in the organization to provide suggestions, criticisms, perceptions, and encouragement. That person can be called a trusted confidant, a mentor, or an angel; but such a relationship should be cultivated and protected because it is invaluable.

CULTIVATING WIDESPREAD SUPPORT

Trainers need to develop support at all levels of an organization. Widespread support is insurance against capricious decisions to end the training efforts in a company. Knowing which people or divisions represent support and which are resistant can help in decision making. With these insights, trainers can consider the needs and desires of supporters and develop strategies about how to influence resisters.

Tolerance is not the same as support. Managers who give lip service to training but are not willing to truly support their employees' attempts to try new skills are not real supporters. True supporters will attend training and urge others to attend. If managers are asked only to support a program, they can easily agree to an ambiguous, nonbinding statement. Therefore, it is often advisable to ask managers and supervisors to assume specific responsibilities rather than just to ask for their tolerant blessing of training programs. They can nominate and work with participants, kick off programs, serve on panels, or help to design or present sessions. In some companies, training is so actively supported that promising managers are rotated through the training function as part of their career development.

Asking senior management to be present at programs, participate in panels, or introduce speakers can increase the credibility of the training function. However, requests of this type should not be frequent enough to impose on senior management, and each person should be carefully chosen for the desired effect.

Developing Relationships

Some programs and projects can be chosen to strengthen relationships with powerful members of an organization. Doing a pet project for a senior vice president can build his or her support of training. Nevertheless, it is important to keep a focus on training and not to get sidetracked by too many projects. A balance must be struck between the political realities of who is asking for a project and the project's impact on the achievement of long-term goals.

Example: Doing projects for powerful organizational members.

Larry, the new manager of training, was busily conducting a needs assessment. Robert, the director of personnel (and an important person in the organization), decided to produce a videotape of the recently enhanced benefits package. When he learned that Larry had been involved in video production in graduate school, he asked him for help with this project. Larry knew the project would be time consuming and would take him away from his main mission of identifying training needs and providing training; but he also recognized the opportunity to build a relationship with a potentially powerful ally, so he helped to produce the video. Robert was thrilled with the product and, at its star-studded preview, publicly complimented Larry. In exchange for about three weeks of work, Larry developed a solid support and increased his visibility and reputation in the organization.

Participants can also be useful allies. If they find programs helpful, they will spread the word, encourage others to attend, and attend other programs themselves. They can also be called on for suggestions and critiques. Participants in some programs may even serve as presenters in other programs.

Although time-consuming, advisory boards can provide support and guidance and can increase the relevance of training efforts. Some organizations have long-standing advisory boards to help to formulate and monitor human resource programs and policies. At other times, advisory groups are gathered to contribute to the design and installation of a specific program (for example, a management-development program).

Using Data to Develop Support

Appropriate and strategic use of evaluation and demographic data can help to increase support for the training function. The key to writing powerful reports lies in carefully tailoring them for chosen audiences. Knowledge of the issues that are important to specific organizational members helps in the collection of appropriate and useful data. Many people fall into one of two extremes regarding data collection and record keeping: (1) Some keep and record every piece of information possible under the assumption that some day they might want it; their offices are crammed full of file cabinets and stacks of paper; and they often have difficulty finding what they do need. (2) Others keep little and are always thereafter wishing they had some long-discarded or never-recorded information. A more moderate approach can have multiple benefits.

The nature and number of reports generated by a training function should be determined during yearly evaluations and needs assessments. Some requests for information are unpredictable; but with careful thought and planning, data that will most likely be needed can be collected through established systems. For example, demographic data regarding the number of participants in programs, the hours and frequency of meetings, and the number of hours that consultants work can routinely be collected as the year progresses. Registration information from program-application forms can become part of a data base that is stored in a computer and used for the preparation of yearly reports. Trying to reconstruct data is a very difficult process. Careful thought and planning can provide exactly what is needed when it is needed.

The trainer alone should not decide what data are to be collected. He or she may consult with senior management or a select group of managers. Planning reports for specific audiences allows the collection of data in the desired formats. For example, the cost per participant for supervisory training might be an interesting statistic for vice presidents of finance and human resources.

To increase the likelihood that a report will be read, the trainer can make it short and focused. Data from evaluation sheets filled out by program participants can be used, and some quotes from their comments about the usefulness of the program can be included. Comparable data from a similar organization and a report explaining the differences and proposing changes are also helpful.

Gaining Productive Visibility

Visibility can be helpful or it can be destructive. Trainers gain one kind of visibility by gathering groups of people together for programs. If the programs are viewed as useful and the trainer does a good job, the visibility will build credibility for the training function. However, exposure through program presentation is not enough; in addition, trainers need to be recognized and appreciated by specific, powerful individuals. As Desatnick writes (1984, p. 46), "High visibility brings with it a challenge: it alone will not bring success. It merely provides the opportunity to succeed—or, conversely, the chance to fail."

Some of the magic of successful visibility lies in the timing of efforts. Robinson (1985, p. 45) writes, "I found overwhelming evidence that an innovator who brought his or her product out at the *right* time was considered a genius. One who introduced the product at the *wrong* time was considered a crackpot."

A trainer's first public efforts are extremely important. The decision about how and where to start (that is, with what programs and what audience) is a strategic decision with many repercussions. The messages about the nature and philosophy of training and development that these choices send to organizational members need to be considered. People notice and remember their first exposure to a new function or a new professional, and sometimes it is hard to alter these impressions.

Gaining productive visibility and building credibility take time. Trainers need to be patient but active during these processes.

SUMMARY

Many decisions about the training function have implications for individuals, departments, and the organization as a whole. Individuals who recognize the political component of their jobs are more likely to be successful and effective in achieving their goals. Careful planning, consultation with a trusted counsel, and knowledge of the environment can increase the likelihood that a training function will be successful.

2

Assessing Needs

Before a training program can be designed, the trainer needs to ascertain what the organization, the unit, or the participants need in the area of training. Developing and conducting needs assessments can generate excitement, creativity, energy, and commitment. Needs assessments are often presented as scientific, quantifiable exercises that provide data to determine the directions of actions and a basis for evaluating successes and failures. Although needs-assessment processes will ideally fulfill both of those goals, they do not have to be highly structured or statistically defendable; they can be thought about in creative and goal-oriented ways as design problems.

A needs assessment can provide opportunities to go out and talk to people—different people from various parts of an organization. The information collected, the ideas generated, and the excitement created when people talk about their work lives can help energize a training effort. The data collected during interviews, by observations, in discussions, or through questionnaires can clarify issues and provide a focus for the training effort.

Although developing and conducting a needs assessment that is tailored for an organization are time-consuming processes, the time investment is essential to the long-term survival of any training function. Brinkerhoff (1986) supports this belief when he writes:

> As HRD practitioners, we must "bother" [to do a needs analysis] because our survival is at stake. In the evolution of a species, unneeded appendages or plumage are selected out and disappear. The same fate may await the HRD profession if *it does not identify, serve, and demonstrate its impact on important organizational needs. In short, we can't afford not to do what is needed or to do what is not needed. (p. 64)*

RATIONALE/OBJECTIVES

There are many beneficial outcomes of thoughtful, well-orchestrated needs assessments, including the following:

1. Increasing the commitment of management and potential participants to training and development;
2. Increasing the visibility of the training function;
3. Clarifying crucial organizational issues;
4. Providing for the best use of limited resources;
5. Providing program and design ideas; and
6. Formulating strategies for how to proceed with training efforts.

Increasing the Commitment of Management

Needs assessments can be designed to provide opportunities for conversations with senior managers about their perceptions of training and development needs and at the same time to provide visibility for trainers in their areas of expertise. Some senior managers are pleased to talk to individuals who are not bringing them problems but are encouraging them to discuss the future and the growth needs of their organizations, two pet interests of many senior people. Because busy managers may have little patience with people who come to talk to them without clarity of focus or a real agenda, trainers can do their homework and be knowledgeable, provide focus, and appear confident, no matter how they might really feel! These meetings can be viewed as chances to increase comfort with and skill in dealing with senior managers. To gain the most in terms of understanding how to deal with these key individuals, trainers need to develop strategies beforehand and analyze the interactions afterward.

Increasing visibility and building a support base with a widespread selection of senior managers are important in a political sense to ensure the future of training efforts. The trainer needs to determine who and how many of the senior people should be interviewed or informed about the needs-assessment process. For example, it is a good idea to consider those who make the decisions concerning financial investments in training and development. However, visibility can be overdone, so careful choices need to be made about whom to contact.

Increasing the Commitment of Potential Participants

When people are part of a process that generates ideas for training programs, there is a greater likelihood that they will be interested in attending those programs or telling others about them. Often individuals who are involved either in a needs assessment or in subsequent programs become committed to the success of training and development efforts. They may stay in contact during the year by submitting ideas, sending articles or cartoons that they think will be useful, or calling to discuss problems that they would like to see addressed in new programs.

Increasing the Visibility of the Training Function

A needs-assessment process can signal a change to members of an organization when a training and development function is either being created or being changed in some significant way.

Example: Using needs assessment to increase visibility of organizational commitment to training and development.

An internal training function was closed down because of financial concerns and changes in senior management. The company had not changed its commitment to providing training but wanted the training efforts to be more cost effective and relevant. An extensive needs-assessment process was designed and conducted, not only to gather information on the types of training that people would find most useful, but also to signal to the community that the organization's commitment to providing development opportunities was as strong as ever. Thus, the needs assessment successfully forestalled the rumor mill.

Example: Using needs assessment to communicate a change in the focus of a training effort.

A man with experience and interest in computer training was hired as the manager of training and development in a large, nonprofit organization. Subsequently many of the training programs had a heavy focus on becoming comfortable with automation. When he left the position, a decision was made to focus less on computer-related training. A new manager was hired, and a needs assessment helped inform the employees of the proposed change in the focus of the training function.

A needs-assessment process should be only as visible as is comfortable and/or appropriate within an organization. If a goal is to let as many employees as possible know that training is going to be available or that the training opportunities are undergoing significant change, the process can be designed for maximum visibility. In this case, in-house newsletters can solicit suggestions for program ideas from those who have not participated in the process formally; or a memo can be sent to all employees, informing them that a needs assessment is being conducted and asking them to participate by submitting their ideas.

Some organizations do not tolerate widespread visibility of change efforts. Managers in some companies believe that change should occur discreetly and without fanfare. Organizational norms should be considered to prevent contrary actions, and trusted counsel can be sought to help in developing the best strategy for informing the community.

Clarifying Crucial Organizational Issues

The literature in training and development is filled with references to the dangers involved in initiating programs on the basis of specific requests from managers. Michalak and Yager (1979) caution about this:

> Warn the unwary trainer that the manager who identifies a problem in the department is often talking about symptoms rather than causes. It would be foolhardy for the trainer to design, develop, and conduct a training program based on the manager's perception of what is needed.
>
> A needs analysis is conducted to identify the causes of the problem. (p. 4)

People often claim that there is a communication problem when they do not understand what is going on in the work place. When people feel frustrated and underused in their jobs, they may say that the organization does not provide career-development opportunities. Reasonable-sounding catch phrases have been the origin of many ill-conceived training programs.

Example: Discrepancy between the presentation of a problem and the real problem.

Frank managed a group that was responsible for facilitating the use of shared technical equipment in a large research and development organization. He told Ann, the company's training director, that there was a communications problem in his department: employees were not following instructions and team spirit was flagging. He wanted to devote some time at their weekly staff meetings to improving communication in the department.

Before agreeing to any training sessions, Ann talked to a cross section of members of the organization. She discovered that Frank had a lot of trouble delegating work and communicating his expectations and that his staff had never felt comfortable enough to give him this feedback. Then she was able to work with Frank and help him to be more effective. His ability to accept responsibility for his part in creating problems and his efforts to change contributed enormously to improving the group's morale. If the training director had taken the manager's original diagnosis as the basis for designing an intervention, the situation might not have improved.

A needs assessment can educate managers about what training can realistically accomplish. As Holt (Condon, 1985) writes:

> When managers run into performance problems, the automatic response is to send the person to training to get fixed. Training may not be the answer. When training is appropriate, the manager needs to understand that the problem is likely to recur when the employee returns to an unaltered work environment that does not support the training. (p. 19)

Training that supports organizational goals and addresses critical business issues in a company will be valued and supported. The more trainers know about the problems of their companies and in their industries, the better the decisions they can make about investing training dollars for impact. As Georgenson and Del Gaizo (1984) say:

> A successful needs analysis identifies the training priorities that help solve an organization's most critical business issues. It helps when making training investment decisions and sorting out those options that will make an impact. It separates training from non-training solutions and identifies the factors or rewards that will support training. A successful needs analysis helps the trainer gain credibility as a professional truly concerned with improving organizational performance. (p. 44)

Providing for the Best Use of Limited Resources

Because budgets are critically reviewed and are sometimes cut, it is important to invest limited resources wisely. Interventions and programs that make the most sense in terms of appropriate payoff for the organization and the participants should be chosen. A trainer can make better decisions regarding training programs if he or she knows what is valued in an organization and what is or is not working well.

Providing Program and Design Ideas

A needs-assessment process can generate program ideas that uniquely represent the nature of an organization.

Example: Using a needs assessment to collect ideas about training programs.

A new manager of training at a technically oriented organization discovered, in a needs-assessment process, that the members of the administrative and support staff often did not understand the nature and breadth of the work conducted in the company. They would pick up major news magazines or Sunday newspapers and see references to the cutting-edge research generated by their company. Technical jargon flourished, but real understanding of the scope of the work was lacking among the support troops. Often employees lost perspective about the importance of their own work because of lack of clarity about the big picture.

The manager of training established a program involving the principal researchers, some of whom were famous scientists, who presented the basic nature of their work in nonscientific language for nontechnical people. The scientists, with a lot of reminding and cajoling, usually accepted the challenge of presenting the meat of their work in a clear, succinct, and jargon-free manner. In addition, many of them communicated contagious enthusiasm for their work. Hearing about frontier research directly from its pioneers was exciting for the staff. The manager of training might never have realized the need for nor the potential effect of this program without conducting the needs assessment.

Needs-assessment processes can generate ideas and examples that can be used to create cases, simulations, and role plays. The more the skills and concepts taught can be brought home by addressing problems that are real to the participants, the more likely it is that the learnings will be retained.

Formulating Strategies for How to Proceed

The data generated during a needs assessment can help in formulating strategies that make sense in an organization. For example, data can be collected to help in deciding if it is more advantageous to concentrate on improving supervisory and managerial skills or to provide programs geared to all levels of employees. Data can be used to determine if employees would prefer short, focused courses or long-term, in-depth programs.

The needs-assessment process can help to identify sources of support and resistance to training. It can be lonely to be the only person or one of just a few people involved in training and development in an organization. Sometimes it is hard to maintain enthusiasm and creativity, especially when the sources of resistance seem stronger than the sources of support. Talking to people in an organization during a needs assessment can be exciting. Generally some of the people believe that training is important; and they contribute new ideas, strategies, different ways of looking at things, and general support. Even talks with those who publicly demean training and development efforts often yield excellent ideas and contribute to the ultimate success of training programs.

When starting a new training effort or changing the function significantly, the trainer will find that the data collected can help with the important decision of which programs to use for a debut. The data can help in answering questions about the best use of limited resources for desired impact. (For example, should a lot of resources be committed to provide supervisory training in order to change the internal environment of the organization, or should the resources be used to improve customer relations and profits?)

A balance needs to be found between the needs identified and the values and goals of a company. Sometimes they are not compatible. Trainers should make decisions with an awareness of differences between personal values and agendas and those of top management.

GOALS

The first step in designing any program involves obtaining clarity about the goals, and the same is true of designing a needs assessment. Before attempting such an assessment, it is a good idea to answer the following questions:

- What should be accomplished by the needs assessment?
- What should be known or clarified at the end of the needs assessment?
- What data should the process generate?
- What expectations/hopes/fears are held about the needs assessment?
- What decisions should be easier to make with the data generated?

Example: Using a needs assessment to identify skill deficits.

A training manager had decided to begin a series of programs for the secretarial staff. She knew what programs were usually well received by this audience but decided to conduct a needs assessment to gain clarity. She made a check list of programs for the secretaries to help her to determine which to offer initially. The woman who typed the list mentioned her interest in programs on stress management and dealing with angry customers. The training manager had not put either program on the list.

The training manager realized that her initial list contained assumptions about what was needed. Therefore, she went back to her office and began to list her reasons for offering programs to the secretarial staff and what she hoped to learn from the needs assessment. She knew that she needed to find out what skill deficits really existed for the secretaries, what tasks they were having trouble with, and what their supervisors wanted them to do differently. She realized that the needs assessment would be more useful if it generated information on (1) what the secretaries really did in their jobs, (2) what tasks caused them difficulty or tempted them to procrastinate, and (3) the managers' perceptions of what training was needed by the secretarial staff. As a result of this increased clarity about what she needed to know, she designed a process that provided useful, relevant data.

To make the best use of limited resources, the trainer can use the needs assessment as a simultaneous means of gathering other types of information. For example, if other people in the organization will be asked to make presentations or to do training in programs that will ultimately be offered, the needs assessment can be used to identify some potential resources. During interviews the trainer can elicit suggestions about who might have the expertise and/or interest in making presentations. This is one way to identify people with hidden expertise (for example, a data-processing director who has led workshops on the topic of "making effective presentations" during professional-association meetings). The trainer should be careful, however, not to raise the expectation that all who are suggested will actually be asked to make presentations.

If interviews are used as part of the needs assessment, questions may be tailored to elicit specific kinds of information. For example, if more women than men apply for training, trainers may ask participants for reasons for this trend. Participants may also be asked for ideas on how to cut costs or how programs that have been offered succeeded in meeting or failed to meet their expectations. Employees who are interviewed or surveyed are potential consumers of training products; they are excellent resources on both their training needs and organizational issues.

Because of the overwhelming quality of unknown processes, many trainers avoid needs assessments. They think that because the programs they offer are filled to capacity and because there are long waiting lists for future programs, they must be on the right track. However, without conducting needs assessments, these professionals might not be using their resources in ways that best fulfill organizational and individual goals.

SUBJECTS

Decisions about who will be included in a needs assessment should take into account the use of people's time and the expense incurred. There is a general belief reflected in the literature that several sources of data are better than just one source (for example, a single group). Those who can be involved in the process include the following:

- Potential participants;
- Former participants;
- Participants' employees;

- Participants' customers or clients;
- Experts on the topic being considered;
- Members of the training department;
- Senior management;
- Volunteers and others expressing interest in being involved; and
- Job-related work groups.

In order to complete a needs assessment within a reasonable time frame, without excessive cost, and without creating a cumbersome process, it is important to consider identified goals and objectives in choosing sources of data. Although it is definitely useful to have input from several sources, input is not usually needed from all possible sources.

The target audience for a needs assessment may be refined so that a sample that is truly representative of that group can be obtained. The nature of the group being sampled must be considered, but the sample may include individuals from large and small departments, people from different parts or geographical locations of the organization, new and long-service employees, men and women, minorities and nonminorities, old and young, professionals and support personnel, people who have been involved in previous training programs and people who have never been involved in training, and so forth. The process may also include those members of senior management with responsibility for the targeted group.

Decisions about who should or should not be included in a needs-assessment process are extremely political ones. Individuals who can provide knowledge of the organization and breadth to the data as well as people who will notice if they are excluded should be included. It is important not to let the needs-assessment process create new resistance or exaggerate existing resistance; knowledgeable and trustworthy counsel can be sought from several sources when making these important decisions.

DATA COLLECTORS

Because a needs assessment is time consuming, the person conducting it might want help in gathering data.

Example: Using available personnel to help to conduct a needs assessment.

A two-person training organization conducted a needs assessment within a large chain of retail stores. With the agreement of the director of personnel, the personnel generalists in the office conducted part of the needs assessment. Usually the generalists went out to the stores to deal with crises and problems. When employees saw them approach, eyebrows would rise in anticipation of their mission.

The needs assessment provided an opportunity for the generalists to go to the stores and talk to employees in a positive rather than crisis-oriented manner. They knew the stores well enough to ensure that a cross section of employees was involved, and they used the process as a chance to talk to people whom they had not previously contacted. Therefore, the generalists increased their relationships within the stores and began interacting in a new mode. It allowed the store employees to see the generalists not only as crisis managers, but also as an expanded resource. While the generalists conducted interviews with employees, the two trainers were able to spend time gathering input from representatives of the various levels of management in the organization. The two trainers could not have completed such a comprehensive needs assessment without the help of the generalists.

If others become involved in conducting interviews, training them can ensure consistency in data collection and simplify efforts to consolidate and analyze the responses. Needs-assessment interviews differ significantly from employment interviews. Therefore, even personnel generalists can benefit from training in the process.

Example: The importance of interviewing skills to the success of a needs assessment.

A training manager involved six line managers in conducting a needs assessment in one division of a company. He was somewhat intimidated by the prospect of supervising their work on the project because they were his peers. A structured-interview format was reviewed with the managers. There was little discussion during that meeting, and the managers began their interviews the next week.

After each manager had conducted six interviews, the training manager asked to look at the data generated. It was apparent immediately that three managers had gathered similar data, two had extremely different data, and one had the data in an entirely different format. From conversations with the managers, the training manager realized that he needed to be much clearer and more directive in explaining how to ask the questions and how to record the answers and in teaching the interviewers not to lead the subjects to supply certain kinds of answers. Because he had looked at the data early in the interviewing schedule, he was able to save the process by stopping it until he had adequately trained the interviewers.

GENERATING ENTHUSIASM AND CREATIVITY

Survey and interview questions are often problem oriented, and they engender gripe sessions and/or reinforce unrealistic expectations. Information can be elicited in ways that will tap people's originality and enthusiasm, and needs-assessment instruments or processes can be fashioned to generate positive solutions and vision-oriented thinking that will help to set a favorable climate. For example, the interviewer might consider the following techniques:

1. ***Ask people to talk about their shining hours in their jobs rather than about the kinds of problems they have.*** Ask them to talk about those times when they thought they had accomplished something or had felt proud of their work, either as individuals or as team members. The discussions that follow this type of questioning can help individuals to get in touch with their positive feelings about their jobs. If respondents are then asked to talk about what prevents such positive experiences from happening more frequently, their perspectives tend to be more solution oriented than when they are asked questions such as "What do you dislike most about your job?"

2. ***Try to create an atmosphere that encourages creativity and new perspectives rather than one that generates familiar answers and confirms existing beliefs.*** Energetic, thoughtful questioning on the part of the trainer increases participants' involvement in and commitment to the training function. Whenever possible, form groups for discussion that allow a difference of opinions and perspectives; try to establish an open, nonjudgmental atmosphere to encourage playfulness and creativity. If participants enjoy being involved in the process, they might continue to contribute ideas and suggestions after the formal needs assessment has been completed.

It is very important not to lead respondents; questions can be asked in ways that do not presuppose a certain kind of answer. Sometimes asking individuals to rank order several potential programs restricts creativity; on the other hand, asking only open-ended questions can overwhelm people and hinder their responses.

OBTAINING USABLE DATA

The trainer needs to think about how the response data will be used and what kinds of responses are likely to be generated by the questions that are posed. Questions can be asked in forms that will allow the data to be distilled, summarized, and analyzed. When designing questions, it is important to consider whether the answers will be useful, whether conclusions can be drawn from them, what else needs to be known, what information will be needed for the kinds of reports desired afterward, and whether baseline data are needed to evaluate the success of subsequent programs.

It is often wise to test questionnaire or interview formats to make sure that people can understand the questions and that the data are being collected in a format that is useful. It is easier to make changes in a format after ten interviews than after fifty.

STARTING A NEEDS ASSESSMENT

Managers need to know if people in their departments will be part of the process and how much time will be required. Individuals need to know whether they will be involved in the process and what will be expected of them. Needs assessments can be very visible and increase organizational awareness of training, or they can be very discreet. The way in which the process is announced should make sense in the organization; for example, a letter signed by a senior manager to inform all personnel about the process would be a highly visible announcement.

CHOOSING DATA-GATHERING METHODS

There are many different methods for collecting data during a needs-assessment process. Decisions about which methods to use should balance economy and appropriateness of design with the realities of organizational life. Knowledge about the successes and failures of previous efforts to gather data within the organization will be helpful. Even though a training and development needs assessment might never have been conducted, it is likely that at some point the organization has undergone a data-gathering process related to benefit choices, policy changes, research questions, and so forth. Information on what went well and what could have been done better during that process can help in planning a needs assessment.

The trainer must decide which approaches to use to gather data. Sometimes a combination of techniques can increase the breadth of the process. Individual interviews, group discussions, anonymous questionnaires sent to past participants, and telephone interviews can be used in the same needs-assessment process. Interviews are more interactive and thus more involving than questionnaires. They can increase people's feelings of being involved in and committed to programs that develop as a result. However, interviewing is very time consuming and exhausting; questionnaires can reach many more people and, thus, increase visibility and exposure. Balance is needed in regard to concerns about which methods will produce the types of data desired, which methods can be implemented with available personnel, and which will be accepted by the subjects and the organization.

Once a needs-assessment effort is started, completing it quickly will help to maintain momentum and build credibility. It is essential to choose formats that can be implemented by the existing staff. For example, a solitary trainer in an organization usually does not have an option of conducting three hundred interviews.

Whatever processes are chosen, the trainer must be careful not to raise people's expectations that everything suggested will be done. Participants should be informed that trends in the data will be identified and addressed.

The following guidelines may be helpful in planning a needs assessment:

- Develop formats that ensure individual anonymity, if that is an organizational issue; and let participants know how their anonymity and confidentiality will or will not be protected.
- Let participants know how the data will be recorded and analyzed.

- Approach the issue of generating formats in the same ways in which the content of the training program is designed.
- Research and read about others' approaches; ask counterparts in other organizations to share their formats and, more importantly, their experiences with the formats.
- Do not be intimidated by highly structured, rigid designs; use what makes most sense in the organization.

The more popular methods used to gather needs-assessment data include the following:

- Studying job content and the skills necessary for successful performance;
- Identifying those areas rated as most important to success in a job;
- Observing job performance;
- Studying data that have been collected in an organization;
- Using questionnaires;
- Conducting interviews; and
- Convening committees or advisory groups to discuss organizational needs.

Job-Content Descriptions

The literature offers suggestions of ways to enumerate the tasks, responsibilities, skills, and abilities that comprise successful job performance. With knowledge of what is needed to do a good job or a group of jobs, trainers can design programs to upgrade the skills of the incumbents and train new employees.

Job content can be ascertained by looking at existing job descriptions and by gathering data from those doing the job. Individual job incumbents may be asked to list their major tasks, to keep lists of how they actually spend their time on the job, or to rate existing lists of major tasks and skills in terms of importance. If standards and gaps in performance are identified, programs may be designed to upgrade necessary skills.

Management may be asked to rank order skills and abilities for groups of jobs. The lists generated may then be compared with the incumbents' proficiencies to identify training needs.

Identification of Crucial Job Skills

Identifying the skills and abilities that are crucial to success in a job can help in choosing the focus of training programs. Zemke (1979) writes about the critical-incident method, a technique that involves asking individuals to talk about times when they were very effective as well as times when they were ineffective in their jobs. Responses are then analyzed, and a list of the factors necessary for success is created. Knowledge of the few skills that are most important allows trainers to use limited resources in effective ways.

Observation

Trainers or trained observers can watch individuals perform their jobs and note the actual skills displayed. Observations of employees who are identified as top performers can generate valuable knowledge of what is necessary for excellence in a job or group of jobs. Establishing standards for effective performance and clarity with regard to the actual skills used on the job can help in the identification of training needs.

Organizational Data

All organizations keep data and records on their employees. Often a review of existing organizational data can yield interesting insights into the kinds of training needed and the potential audiences for training. The kinds of numerical data routinely kept in many organizations include numbers of absences by department; numbers and categories of employees leaving, being fired, and being hired; turnover rates by department; and productivity records. Other kinds of data that may prove useful are performance-review and exit-interview documents.

Many organizations generate statements about missions, trends, and policies in a variety of formats, including strategic plans, speeches and statements by senior management, and annual reports. Reading documents produced for company-wide or public-oriented distribution can help in clarifying future training needs and areas of transition for employees. When trainers are aware of trends and goals, they can produce programs that are more responsive to their organizations.

Questionnaires

Questionnaires are often used as part of a needs-assessment effort. They can take many forms—from one sentence on a sheet of paper to complex, computer-analyzed formats. Creating a questionnaire is similar to designing any instrument. The designer must be careful to create one that will generate the kinds of data desired. In order for the questionnaire to be effective, considerable thought must be given to what the answers will mean and what can be done with those data.

The way in which questions are written can influence the result. Therefore simple, jargon-free language should be chosen. The designer can word questions in ways that do not influence the reader toward one kind of response and that do not lead to unrealistic expectations about what will occur as a result of the needs-assessment process.

A questionnaire should be only as long as is necessary to obtain the information desired. It is generally a good idea to use a variety of kinds of questions (for example, true-false, short answers, and multiple choice) to hold respondents' interest and to provide the best chance of obtaining accurate and complete data. If the questionnaire includes a check list of the skills required to do a job, respondents may be asked to check off those skills or areas of knowledge in which training is needed.

A scale may be used by respondents for the purpose of ranking their responses on an item (for example, "Rank your satisfaction with the following on a scale from 1 to 5, where 1 means not at all satisfied and 5 means completely satisfied"). However, because people interpret the distances between such numbers quite differently, drawing conclusions from the rankings is difficult without base-line data with which to compare results. It may be more effective to name all the points on a scale rather than just naming the end points (for example, "1 means terrible, 2 means poor but I can live with it, 3 means it is O.K.").

Another way to compare items is to ask respondents to rank order items in relationship to one another. For example, respondents may be asked to rank a list of training programs in order of their usefulness in increasing effectiveness on the job (that is, they may be asked to place a 1 next to the item that has the highest priority, a 2 next to the item with the next-highest priority, and so on).

More open-ended formats may also be used. Respondents may be asked, "What kinds of training would help you to be more effective in your job?" Berdie and Anderson (1974, p. 62) note the importance of giving thought to how a questionnaire begins: "The subject's first impression of the questionnaire is all important; based on this impression he may decide to either complete or not complete the form. Therefore, start the questionnaire with interesting yet nonthreatening items."

Spitzer (1979) suggests that well-written cover letters and incentives for promptly completing questionnaires may help to increase the response rate. Berdie and Anderson (1974, p. 67) stress persistence in follow-up efforts: "Rarely has a questionnaire survey achieved acceptable response rates without the use of follow-up procedures." They then warn, "Remember, persistence does not mean obnoxiousness. Let your nonrespondents realize that their response is missed and really desired."

Interviews

Interviews may be conducted in person, on the telephone, with a single individual, or in a group. They may be free-wheeling discussions; they may be based on some open-ended questions; they may be guided by a few specified areas of concern; or they may be highly structured. Needs-assessment interviews often consist of questions about job content and responsibilities, job satisfaction and performance, the kinds of training that respondents would find helpful in being more effective or more satisfied in their jobs, the respondents' history of job-related training, retrospective evaluation of past training experiences, and projections of trends or future needs for training.

Interviews may be kept fresh by the development of alternate questions to generate the same kinds of data; using this approach helps to renew the interviewer's enthusiasm and originality. This approach also helps to maximize the interactive nature of the interviews while providing data that can easily be synthesized. For example, many interview formats include questions concerning job content; different kinds of questions could elicit similar responses to this topic. Any of the following requests or questions could generate useful data on job content:

- Describe your responsibilities.
- What kind of work do you do each day?
- Identify the most important things that you do in your job.
- If you were leaving your job and were talking to your replacement, what parts of the job would you be sure to talk about?
- What types of items do you usually cross off your to-do list each week?
- What parts of your job are unique to your position?
- What parts of your job are central to the purpose of your office?

Sometimes in-depth interviews are conducted after administration of a questionnaire to clarify priorities and generate areas for discussion. Zemke and Walonick (1980, p. 89) state that most questionnaires do not provide enough useful information and that "interviews, focus groups, site visits, and reviews of performance data all help you clarify and define the goal of your study and give you a context for explaining the results."

Advisory Groups

In an effort to involve members of the community, to generate support, and to tap available expertise and interest, advisory groups are sometimes formed as part of a needs-assessment process. Such groups can discuss perceived needs, represent constituencies, and decide on priorities. Clearly, a choice to create an advisory group has implications. The composition of the group, responsibilities, authority, and reporting relationships are a few of the issues that must be considered.

Sometimes in-depth interviews are conducted after administration of a questionnaire to clarify priorities and generate areas for discussion. Zemke and Walonick (1980, p. 89) state that most questionnaires do not provide enough useful information and that "interviews, focus groups, site visits, and reviews of performance data all help you clarify and define the goal of your study and give you a context for explaining the results."

Advisory Groups

In an effort to involve members of the community, to generate support, and to tap available expertise and interest, advisory groups are sometimes formed as part of a needs-assessment process. Such groups can discuss perceived needs, represent constituencies, and decide on priorities. Clearly, a choice to create an advisory group has implications. The composition of the group, responsibilities, authority, and reporting relationships are a few of the issues that must be considered.

Establish an Ongoing Process

Many people conceive of needs assessments as singular and discrete efforts to gather information. It is a better use of time and effort to design a needs assessment as a process that sets up relationships and provides information in an ongoing fashion. This can be accomplished by establishing a network of people who can continue to provide information and ideas for developing programs in order to keep training and development efforts current and in contact with changes in the world of work. Systems also need to be established to keep the trainer in touch with those individuals who provided data during the initial needs-assessment process; contacting them periodically for new insights and ideas is helpful. When individuals start to think of training as a possible solution to problems that arise, they begin to see the training function as a resource—a place to start—when they want answers or a sounding board. Some of this change in their consciousness is a result of the increased visibility and accessibility of training resources, and the change begins with their involvement in a needs-assessment process.

ANALYSIS

Analyzing the Data

A well-conceived needs assessment will provide a great deal of useful data, but the information generated must be distilled into manageable results that make sense to the trainer and ultimately to the organization. Depending on the type of data collected, different methods of analysis are typically used. Elaborate statistical analysis is not usually necessary, and the following paragraphs present several simple methods of analysis that can provide a basis for understanding the data better.

Frequency Counts

Counting the number of responses to a given question may be sufficient in some cases (for example, reporting the number of respondents who answered yes to a question). For ease in comparison, the percentage of the total number of respondents can be calculated.

Means, Modes, and Medians

Very basic arithmetic calculations can provide three useful statistics. The *mean* is the average response. It is found by adding all the scores and dividing the total by the number of responses. The *mode* is the one score that occurs most frequently. It is found simply by examining all of the scores and determining which one occurs most often. Sometimes more than one score will be the mode. The *median* is the score in the middle (that is, there are equal numbers of respondents with scores larger than the median and smaller than the median). Comparing the results of these three types of analyses can yield interesting results. Zemke and Walonick (1980) emphasize the usefulness of graphing the three results, if they are quite different, to see how they are skewed.

Content Summaries

Open-ended questions and interviews yield data that are not easily condensed, and it can be helpful to group the responses into categories. Interview data should be transformed into transcripts or notes; then the notes can be read and the major themes listed. Going through the data again and dividing the responses among themes or categories will allow new groupings to emerge. It may help to photocopy the actual questionnaires or interview notes and literally cut up the responses and place them in piles representing different content areas. Using this technique allows comments to be easily moved and shifted around until the most useful groupings are discovered. The actual responses may then be summarized.

The aim of comment analysis is to reduce the content areas while retaining a sense of the nature of the comments. Content summaries can provide frequency counts of the number of responses in a given content area and examples of the types of comments generated.

Intuition

People doing analyses must not underestimate the importance of results that jump out at them while they are looking at the responses. Zemke and Walonick (1980, p. 91) write about the "interoccular trauma test": if results hit the reader between the eyes, they probably have practical importance.

GENERATING COMPREHENSIBLE FORMATS

The data should be recorded in usable formats so that they can be easily understood and interpreted six months or a year after completion. Compatible formats are essential if the data will be compared to data generated elsewhere in the organization or by another training organization. Data should always be recorded in ways that can be reported to and understood by others.

Interpreting Results

It is tempting to read causes and effects and desired outcomes into data. The interpreter should try to be objective, state clearly what was found, and not report conjectures as if they were based on fact. Results should be viewed and used for what they say and what they support or question, not for more than they say.

USING THE DATA GENERATED

After distilling and summarizing the information collected, it is helpful to answer the following questions:

- What trends are evident in the data?
- Who is asking for what kind of training and development opportunities?
- Where should limited resources be invested for the greatest payoff?
- What directions should be taken in planning?

Political implications of trends in the data can be considered, and decisions about how to proceed can be made on the basis of desired outcomes. Knowledge of respondents' attitudes and organizational values will help in dealing with issues such as the following:

- Should programs focus on job-related skills only, or can some programs have a personal-growth focus?
- Should different types of programs be available for individuals from different organizational levels?
- How many programs should initially be offered?
- Who are the audiences? Should programs be offered on a volunteer basis to the organization at large or to select departments as teams?
- Should permanent, rotating, or program-related advisory groups be used to help in planning and designing programs?
- How important is it to appear as if the training and development effort is not costing a lot? Is it an issue of keeping real costs low or of looking cost conscious?

Example: Keeping appearances consistent with organizational values.

A training director of a large educational organization attended a regional conference with her supervisor, the director of personnel. At a round-robin session, the director of personnel talked about the program booklet that had been developed and disseminated to all employees that year. He emphatically explained how inexpensive the booklet was in comparison with similar efforts by other institutions. Since cost consciousness was a hot

*issue at her institution and the booklet was to have wide visibil-
ity, the training director had created a booklet that looked and
was inexpensive. With great pride her supervisor compared this
booklet with the slick products of the competition.*

The trainer can map out short-term and long-term plans and
check with senior management for consistency. When establishing
a training function, he or she can use the data generated to choose
first efforts. The importance of what is chosen for a debut must not
be underestimated. Clarity of goals, priorities, and direction can help
in choosing successful first efforts.

FOLLOW-UP

The trainer can strengthen credibility and show appreciation by
recontacting everyone who participated in the assessment process
with a report of the findings and the resulting plans. People who
have been asked to invest time and thought in generating information will welcome information about how their input was used. Giving them this information will encourage them to continue to contribute ideas and suggestions and will increase their awareness of,
and commitment to, training and development programs. In addition, this is a political issue; thought must be given to how much
and which information should go to whom. There may be some information that should be shared with senior management before
it becomes general knowledge. Trusted counsel can help in forming a thoughtful strategy for using the information to raise commitment and awareness rather than to cause discomfort and
embarrassment.

Existing channels (for example, regularly scheduled staff
meetings, in-house newsletters, and memos) may be used to communicate the data and plans. The information can be released in
ways that create positive excitement, visibility, and interest.

A major reason to create a needs assessment as a process, rather
than as a single, data-gathering incident, is that a process leads to
a network of individuals who can be recontacted each year for feedback and new ideas. The network can be used to keep programs
responsive and current.

Periodically contacting all past program participants for a
retrospective evaluation of the worth and effect of programs can be

extremely helpful. Past participants also may be asked for their suggestions for other programs. Networks may be created to provide information that will help the trainer to stay aware of changes and trends in the work place. It is important to let the originator know when an idea is developed further or if, for example, a cartoon that was submitted is used in a program. Also, it is a good idea to send a letter, with a copy to the person's supervisor, acknowledging the help.

The effort put into designing and running a needs assessment provides a foundation on which to build successful and inventive programs.

3

Designing Training Sessions

In most professions there are some activities that almost defy description or, at least, are not completely quantifiable. The processes used to design training programs involve this type of mystique. During interviews conducted by the author, many trainers qualified their contributions by stating at the beginning that they were not aware of how they designed programs. Perhaps because most people do not learn a logical sequence or a step-by-step method, they have trouble identifying their own processes. Of course, once the author began talking with those being interviewed, many methods, issues, guidelines, recommendations, cautions, and warnings emerged. Trainers are sometimes paralyzed by the belief that they need to create something entirely novel for the design of a workshop to be worthwhile. Many factors determine whether a design accomplishes what it was meant to do, and originality and uniqueness play relatively tiny parts. As Abella (1986, p. xii) writes, "Excellence in training programs is the result of a dash of inspiration up front and a lot of organization, thoroughness and attention to details in bringing the inspiration to its final form."

This chapter focuses on the process of designing training programs and factors that influence success. Subsequent chapters focus on methods and evaluation of training.

CLARITY OF PURPOSE

The impetus to design a program can come from several sources. Sometimes an assessment process identifies a specific area of need that can best be addressed by a training program. Sometimes management wants a certain program, and it becomes prudent to provide that program. Whatever the origin of the need, it is extremely important to have as much specific information as possible to guide the planning process. The clearer the goals of a program are, the easier it is to choose the most relevant content and to design a useful program. If the original needs-assessment process did not provide information to clarify the focus of a program, it is worth the effort to conduct a mini-needs assessment before investing time in program design. Short interviews, either in person or on the telephone, can be designed to elicit specific, program-related information. Potential participants, their supervisors, and their employees can provide information about what content to include in a program.

Example: Using supervisors of potential participants to clarify program content.

A manager of training and development was designing a program for new supervisors. She met with small groups of senior administrators to discuss plans for the new program. The administrators, many of whom had been with the company for years, had all managed first-line supervisors. During the meetings the administrators were asked to talk about pitfalls they had seen new supervisors fall into, that is, typical problems experienced by those new to supervision. The resulting discussions provided information about potential content for the program and specific ideas for case studies. As an added benefit, the same administrators were among the first to urge new supervisors to attend the program.

The program designer can ask potential participants and/or their supervisors about workshop outcomes. Questions about what participants should be able to do or to do differently after the workshop can yield useful information about program design. Sometimes, during program-related mini-assessments, refinements in audience composition occur. With the additional information gained, programs can be tailored for added relevance.

Example: Clarifying who needs training.

A trainer in an insurance company was asked to design a stress-management program for the secretarial staff. A manager in one of the departments had gathered a list of issues to be covered, and the trainer began to design a program to address them. As he worked on the program, it became clear that he needed to

talk to some secretaries. After talking to a dozen people, he real-
ized that most of the stress was a result of inadequate super-
vision. Secretaries received infrequent performance feedback
and little support during high-volume times. The trainer real-
ized that the emphasis should be on improving the supervision
of the secretarial staff.

Decisions about the audience influence program content, design, and marketing strategy. For example, because the time-management problems of the supervisory personnel are different from those of the secretarial staff, separate time-management programs for the two groups might be more relevant. Also, employees might be hesitant to attend a program on assertive communications if they know that their supervisors could be participants in the same program. Individuals generally feel more comfortable participating with those whom they perceive as peers, particularly in programs encouraging increased self-awareness and attempting to build trust.

Before tackling the development of a program, it is a good idea to write general goals and to try to be as clear and as specific as possible. Behavior-oriented objectives can be written only when there is a clear picture of direction.

Example: Goals for an assertive-communications workshop.

The following goals might be appropriate:

- *Increasing awareness of the differences among asser-*
  tive, aggressive, passive-aggressive, and passive
  behavior;
- *Increasing awareness of the participants' patterns of*
  behavior, fantasies, and physical sensations about these
  styles of interacting;
- *Increasing awareness of the options of behavior and the*
  choices connected with these options;
- *Providing a safe environment for sharing, experimenta-*
  tion, and support; and
- *Encouraging participants to share their knowledge of*
  and experience with assertiveness.

An example of a more specific, behavior-oriented objective for a given session of the above-described workshop could be "providing an opportunity for participants to practice saying 'no' to unreasonable requests."

Time spent in the early stages of the design process, zeroing in on the most useful and relevant directions, can increase participants' interest, commitment, and ability to transfer learning to the work place.

PARTICIPANT INVOLVEMENT IN THE PLANNING PROCESS

There are benefits and liabilities to be considered in deciding who should be involved in the development of a training program. Most trainers agree that to increase relevance it is best to obtain data from some of the people for whom the program is being created. Opinions differ, however, as to how involved participants need to become.

The actual program will often be more useful if content expertise within an organization is tapped. Although the trainer is a specialist in the learning process, he or she is not necessarily an expert in the content area of a program. It is often important to acknowledge that lack of expertise when designing a program and to call on someone in the organization who can provide it. Zemke (Gall, 1986) cautions trainers about this problem:

> It's important to draw from the population that attends the course to find out if, in fact, it is doing what it should or if it just sounds good to you because you don't know anything. I think that's a real danger, if you're not an expert. If you feel you are being personally educated by the course, it's real tempting to assume that it works to educate your audience, who is usually above your level of knowledge in that area. (p. 23)

Using individuals or a group to establish and review the nature and focus of program content can help to ensure accuracy of focus. Individuals can help in the identification of the specific skills that a program should address.

Example: Using individuals in the work place to identify program content.

A trainer was given the assignment of designing a program on job-related interpersonal communication. She developed a list of the skills that she thought needed to be addressed by the program. She met with individuals who worked in the department and asked them (1) to review the list, (2) to add other skills that needed to be addressed and delete those that were not needed, (3) to discuss which three skills they thought were most critical to working successfully with people in their area, and (4) to tell her about two situations from their experience when the lack of (or the possession of) an interpersonal-communication skill caused (or helped in the resolution of) a difficult situation. The information generated by the interviews helped her to identify and choose the program focus.

Some trainers recommend establishing an official design committee to work on program development. Nadler (1976a, p. 3) states that an "effective workshop is best designed by a variety of persons who can each contribute to the development of the design." He suggests that the composition of the committee be representative of anticipated participants who can recommend, react to, or decide about program design. In addition, he warns that successful use of a committee depends on the existence of clear expectations between the coordinator and committee members. Committee functions might include developing workshop objectives, identifying appropriate participants, determining the design, and selecting the site. He cautions that members need to be clear about their role for each function (for example, whether they are to recommend, react to, or decide on each issue).

It is important to know something about the norms and culture of the organization in which the program will take place. Even though two departments may need programs with similar content focus, the designs of the programs might need to be subtly or even radically different, depending on what is accepted and expected behavior in each department.

Example: Effect of organizational norms on program success.

A trainer who was new to the company was assigned the development of a program on delegation for a group of research scientists. He had led a similar workshop in his previous job. After conducting a series of interviews, he decided that the content needed was also similar to that of his previous workshop. Therefore, he did not redesign the workshop but simply tailored it a bit and used it.

The original design included an activity in which participants worked in small groups and came to a consensus on how to delegate several projects among a fictitious staff. Although in its previous use the activity had generated a wonderful discussion, the research scientists did not become involved.

When the trainer realized that the participants were not discussing the delegation activity, he reconvened the total group and tried to find out what the problem was. Finally, it emerged that the participants had jobs in which they rarely worked in teams or groups of any kind. Typically, they had their own individual projects and they worked alone on them. If the trainer had given each participant the same problem to solve individually, they could have subsequently discussed how they made their decisions because they were accustomed to justifying and explaining their own decisions. They just were not comfortable with decision making in small groups with their peers.

Whether a committee is used or individuals are interviewed, involving anticipated audience members in the design process results in a check on relevance and completeness as well as an increased interest in and commitment to the program. It also provides needed content expertise and credibility.

During program-related data collection, problems may emerge other than those that realistically can be addressed by a training program. A conscientious trainer must make some decisions about how to deal with knowledge of problematic issues in the work place. Clearly, decisions of this nature have political implications. A trainer must respect confidentiality; however, if issues emerge in discussions with employees, often the trainer can present them to management without identifying their individual sources. A trainer needs strategies about how, when, and to whom information about problems is relayed. Without making accusations, raising defensiveness, or delving into things that might well be out of line, a trainer needs to think through a plan of action and not just react excitedly to the discovery of new information. This is a time for consultation with a trusted confidant and/or a manager.

DESIGN ORIGIN

Gaining clarity about the purpose, focus, and content of a projected program is only part of the process. Decisions must be made about where the design will come from. The same issues are involved whether an external consultant is hired to design and present the program, a commercially produced program is bought, an existing program is tailored, or a new program is created.

Time is one critical factor in the decision about who will design a program. It is time consuming to find appropriate and reputable consultants and to brief them so that they can design a tailored program; similarly, using internal resources to create a unique program takes time. It is important to make decisions that use time in a manner that is consistent with priorities. If the program has a high priority for the trainer or the organization and if, in all likelihood, there will be additional requests for very similar programs, it makes sense to invest time in creating that program. The payoff will be increased expertise and experience with the content area. It is important to allow enough time to become comfortable with the content so that creative thoughts can be brought to the design. A rushed design process makes it difficult for the trainer to feel totally confident about the product.

Another issue to consider is cost, and there are many ways to think about it. As Newstrom (1975) points out, program cost involves both the initial development of a program and each subsequent administration of that program. Cost can be figured per participant or per program. Either way, the cost changes with the number of times a program is repeated. If a program is very specific, requires specialized expertise, and is geared toward a small segment of the population, it might cost less to hire an outside consultant who possesses the necessary expertise than to require the trainer to become educated on the subject. If the program is to be repeated many times, the resulting cost might justify educating the trainer. The issue of priorities in the use of trainer time also enters into the decision.

Some training functions have no funds to hire external consultants and, therefore, must carefully choose a very small number of programs to design internally. Interests, skills, and development needs are factors to be considered in deciding whether to personally design and/or present a program. Some programs may be particularly seductive because they are based on topics that fit closely with a trainer's values or abilities. Although it is important to consider this aspect in order to generate interesting, involving work and to prevent burnout, this need must be balanced by organizational needs and priorities.

The availability of commercial products for review will determine how easy it is to incorporate them into a program design. For example, if time is quite limited and preview copies of films must be ordered from film companies, it might not be possible to use them. With access to good libraries, preview screening resources, and cooperative colleagues, many existing products can be incorporated into or adapted for training designs.

To avoid reinventing the wheel each time, it is a good idea to review what has already been produced by looking at brochures about similar programs or at the actual materials used. However, there is a difference between using existing materials to generate ideas and plagiarizing them. Although it can be validating to see that many commercially offered programs include similar areas of content, it is another matter to attend a program available to the general public and then reproduce the handouts for use without proper permission. Some companies and individuals are quite willing to allow use of their materials; however, the trainer should always contact the owner or the copyright holder for permission.

Colleagues can provide information about products that they have used, and trainers in other organizations can give their opinions on why a product was successful or unsuccessful in their companies. As Lifton (Gall, 1986) points out:

> I also think maintaining a close relationship with your peers in the training community, to find out what they're doing, is helpful. In the brokerage community in New York City, we have a group of trainers that meets periodically to discuss information that is not proprietary. We feel free to call each other and ask how someone else has done a certain type of training. (p. 25).

There are a number of political implications involved in decisions about who should design and/or present a specific program. One issue concerns visibility. Although the training function is usually seen as responsible for failures or "near misses"—whether or not an external consultant produces the program—sometimes successes are not credited as quickly when those responsible are absent from the actual event. If an external person presents a program, he or she is sometimes given most of the credit. An internal trainer who presents a successful program is seen as a more valuable resource by the participants and by management; he or she has an opportunity to establish stronger relationships with, and more accessibility to, those who participate and their managers. Again, priorities must be considered. If the potential audience is one with which more direct contact is desired and if the program involves familiar content, it might make more sense for the program to be produced and presented by internal training staff. On the other hand, there may be times when less association with an event may be desired (for example, a pilot program that is highly controversial). At those times, use of external presenters and "canned" programs may be better.

Sometimes, without actually presenting a program, a trainer can still appear very involved by conducting well-chosen, predesign interviews; attending the event; introducing the presenters; and chatting with participants at coffee breaks.

Example: Using a program to increase visibility.

After one year with the company, the director of training recognized a need for a new management-development program. Many middle and upper-level managers were hesitant to attend existing programs for fear of seeming unsure of their skills and expertise. The director of training wanted to establish a program that would be highly recognized and that would be a status symbol so that these same managers would not want to be left out and miss the visibility and recognition that attendance would bring. He arranged a series of presentations by senior management on hot company issues.

Because many of the middle and upper-level managers had limited opportunities to interact with these senior people, they were interested in attending. The entire series was marketed as a program specifically designed for middle and upper-level managers on current trends and issues. The program literature implied that participants would benefit most if they were competent and knowledgeable managers to begin with, and that, in fact, a solid management background was necessary to understand the implications of the issues addressed.

The director of training made arrangements for the sessions, introduced the speakers, attended the sessions, and chatted with participants at coffee breaks. It offered him an opportunity to work with many senior, middle, and upper-level managers. His wide visibility in introducing the senior managers increased his credibility and exposure in the company.

PROGRAM CONTENT

When a program is designed internally, it is very important for the trainer to become familiar with the content area of the program and to gain a conceptual framework of the breadth and depth of the field of information that the program could cover. In order to make decisions about what to include and what to exclude, the trainer needs some appreciation of the content area.

All of the trainers who were interviewed by the author about their processes of design discussed this stage. They talked about depending on their basic curiosity about learning new things and their varying degrees of skill in doing library research and informational interviewing. Knowing when to stop this stage of the design process is as important as knowing how to do it. Some people love reading books and articles on a new topic and enjoy talking to experts and, therefore, have difficulty recognizing when they are becoming overwhelmed with information. The amount of research, reading, and discussion that is needed for a new program depends on the nature of the program. When a program is a short introduction for novices, less information is needed than when the program is intended to provide a comprehensive briefing on an issue. If the topic of the program lends itself to self-discovery and using the program participants' expertise, then probably there is less need for a significant contribution of content. In the latter case, more time must be spent on designing ways to promote useful discussion and increase awareness than on library research about content.

Finding sources that relate specifically to the goals, objectives, and audience will save time during the research stage. It is not necessary or wise to try to read everything written on a subject; the articles or chapters that are most relevant are usually sufficient. Informed decisions can be made by choosing key areas of content that relate most closely to the context of the audience and the organization. Business-school libraries are a good source, especially if the trainer makes an effort to become acquainted with the research librarians. The trainer might find it useful to learn to do computer-literature searches. A well-worded search can turn up resources on a very specific topic or can help to limit an extensive content area. Attending programs on unfamiliar topics, watching other trainers work, seeing what content they choose to emphasize, and gaining a sense of the concepts and issues involved can also help in developing subsequent programs.

If information is gathered and cataloged, some can be used later in lecturettes, some can be used in handouts, and some will provide frameworks or models. Information may be collected in whatever manner works, for example, writing on index cards or legal-sized pads, cutting up photocopies, using computer outlining systems, or typing one's notes. The important aspect is to try to grasp a sense of the groups or categories of information that exist on a topic and to group the notes or photocopies accordingly. For example, readings on time management yield information on how to handle interruptions and paperwork, how to stop procrastination, and common time wasters. When readings begin to yield less and less new information, it is probably time to stop the research phase and to try to consolidate the information.

PROGRAM FORMAT

At some point in the design phase, attention must be shifted from the content of the program to the process. Sometimes individuals stall in the research phase because they are stymied in their decisions about how to build a learning experience. It is fairly straightforward to organize a talk or a lecture; but current theories of adult learning suggest the importance of providing opportunities for learning that are varied, involving, and experiential and that capitalize on the expertise of the participants. Decisions about a number of issues can guide this part of the design process, and the following paragraphs discuss some of these issues.

Different Learning Styles

The participants in most training programs are adults and come to the training session with years of experience as learners. On one hand, these participants create a situation in which there is a lot of expertise and life experience that can be drawn on to create an involving learning session. On the other hand, however, the participants may be very aware of how they learn best and may be impatient with situations that do not specifically address their needs.

During the design phase, it is important to remain aware of addressing the needs of participants with different learning styles. For example, if participants need to understand a difficult concept, overhead projectors may be used for those who learn best visually; handouts, for those who prefer to read; lectures, for those who learn by listening; and small-group discussions, for those who need to talk about a concept in order to learn it. If the ways in which information is presented are varied, each participant will be able to obtain some of the learning by using his or her best learning style. Also, opportunities for participants to share their knowledge and experience can be devised.

Every trainer has a preferred style of learning and of presenting information. It is important to be aware of one's preferences and not to allow them to limit the participants' opportunities to learn. For example, some trainers do not feel comfortable with the unpredictability of group discussions; consequently, they design mostly small-group discussions to avoid answering questions from the group at large. Although this type of design provides opportunities for people to engage in conversation, it does not allow common group themes to emerge with as much clarity as they might, does not give participants access to the expertise of individuals in other groups, and does not offer the total group the chance to hear the same answers to questions that arise. Devising a design that varies the styles of content presentation will prevent the trainer's own style preferences from monopolizing the program.

Creating Readiness

Adult learners come to training situations with preconceptions, based on their own experiences, about what will happen and what will be expected of them. It is extremely important to be aware of this fact and to prepare participants by increasing their receptivity and readiness. Programs should be advertised honestly and described as clearly as possible with lists of realistic objectives and outcomes. Prospective participants can make informed decisions about whether and how to be involved if they are told beforehand about the content of the training, the format, what they can realistically expect to gain from participation, and what they will be asked to do. Individuals who come to a workshop expecting the same kind of learning experience that they had in school often have difficulty becoming involved in a more participatory environment.

Prework can help participants to develop realistic expectations about the focus and projected outcomes of a workshop and can prepare them to participate more fully. For example, participants' prework may take the form of completing questionnaires about why they are coming to the workshop and what they want to accomplish. The participants may also be asked to give copies of their completed questionnaires to their supervisors. Figure 1 offers an example of a preprogram work sheet.

TRAINING & DEVELOPMENT
PREPROGRAM WORK SHEET

_____   _____
           Program Title   Program Date

Instructions: Please review and complete the questions below with your supervisor, referencing the program objectives in the Training & Development Guide.

1. The following are work situations in which I want to improve my skills.

2. As a result of this program, I want to achieve the following:

3. Any other related information:

_____   _____   _____
  Signature of Participant   Signature of Supervisor   Date

Requirements for Program Attendance. To help ensure your learning and use of new skills:
   BRING one copy of this form to the program.
   GIVE one copy to your supervisor.
   SEND one copy to Training & Development, *at least five days before the program.*

Figure 1. Example of a Preprogram Work Sheet[1]

---

[1]Reprinted with the permission of Analog Devices in Norwood, Massachusetts.

One note of caution should be observed: before supervisors agree to allow employees to attend a workshop, they should be informed of expectations about participants' involvement in activities before, during, and after that workshop. Supervisors cannot be expected to be involved willingly without prior knowledge and agreement. When supervisors know about participants' expected time commitments in advance, they might choose to have their employees attend programs at more convenient times of the year.

Involving participants in prework helps to start the learning process early and extends the impact of the workshop. As Connellan (Gall, 1986, p. 22) writes, "They need to start the digestion process. The sooner you get people thinking the better chance you have of great ideas germinating."

The way in which a program actually begins creates expectations and sets a climate. From the moment when participants enter the room, their initial experiences set the stage for how they will engage in the processes that follow. A trainer can establish the norms for a program directly or indirectly. For example, at the beginning of the program, he or she can lead a discussion of ground rules, including the expectation that there will be extensive participation. In contrast, a trainer can choose to raise the issue less directly by involving participants in a small-group activity as soon as they come into the room, thereby immediately creating a norm of active participation.

Flow of Design

The structure of the training design can greatly affect how participants feel about the learning process. The flow of the design from one activity or experience to another can have as many variations as outcomes and can influence the climate of the workshop. It can help people to feel involved and connected, or it can cause them to feel confused and isolated.

When considering the design and flow of a workshop, it can help to be clear about any secondary goals that may exist. For example, if a secondary goal is to create a team feeling among participants, a team may be built through the workshop design. Early in the process the participants may work individually; later they may work in small groups; and finally, near the end of the process, they may become involved in some total-group experiences. Or, if one of the goals of the workshop is to increase networking in the organization, the design of the session may give participants the opportunity to work in a number of different small groups in which they can meet many other individuals. If a goal is to increase comfort with self-disclosure, intimacy and trust may be built by creating small groups that stay together for the duration of a workshop.

Maintaining an awareness of the balance between the content presented in a session and the process of the session is one of a trainer's most difficult jobs. Each session is based on information or content that has been designated as important to the participants and to accomplishing program objectives. At the same time, a trainer needs to pay attention to how individuals and the group as a whole are functioning.

When designing a workshop, the trainer can test the flow by trying to imagine how it would feel to be a participant. Because different participants may prefer different styles of presentation, there is no need to be hesitant about repeating important content in several formats. This is particularly important when giving instructions for an activity. If there is a way to misunderstand, some participant will find it. Therefore, instructions should be tested ahead of time, perhaps with colleagues or friends. It is possible to present and explain instructions in several ways or to give a number of examples and still treat participants like adults.

It is difficult to know how well a workshop will work. The first time a new design is presented, it is hard to predict the time required for activities, the extent of participant involvement, the amount of discussion that will be generated, the number of questions that will be raised, and whether the design will aid the learning process. Each time a workshop is repeated, the change in the overall composition of the participant group and in the interaction of participants with one another will make it difficult to predict outcomes. Decisions about how structured or unstructured to make a workshop are influenced by the trainer's comfort with flexibility. New trainers tend to overdesign; they try to include too much content in a session. It is a good idea to think through alternatives and additions to a design in advance, but these elements may be thought of as options. Timing and the prediction of timing are extremely difficult concepts to master. The more comfortable that trainers become in working with groups, the more willing they are to underdesign or to be flexible with the structures they have prepared. This strategy is more risky, but it can allow for spontaneous learning and experimentation.

Cues from participants can help in determining whether a program is running smoothly. If participants are not following directions, are spontaneously chatting with one another at inappropriate times (that is, when they are supposed to be working individually, listening to a lecturette, or involved in a large-group discussion), or are confused and irritated, any of these signs may indicate a problem. When a trainer begins to feel annoyed because the design is not working or because the participants are not cooperating, it may be time to stop the process. An unscheduled break can be taken to provide time for deciding what to do next or for checking with participants about what is happening. It is possible that a program is not exactly on target or that the participants have received disconcerting news. A trainer who feels comfortable in sharing his or her own feelings and confusion can do so and can also ask participants what they are experiencing. After gathering such data and taking an unscheduled break, the trainer can formulate a new strategy for the rest of the program. It is important to let the participants know what has been decided and why.

There is a world of difference between being unprepared and being flexible enough to use design options. No one benefits when the trainer is unprepared. When the trainer has not given forethought to goals, objectives, content, and design structure, participants flounder and often lose focus. Although participants sometimes complain that trainers are too rigid and wedded to their design structures and thus are unable to help the group to learn, they do not complain that trainers are too well prepared. Maintaining workable balances between structure and flexibility, between the focus on content and the focus on process, and between spontaneity and control of timing requires skills that rapidly increase with experience. Watching more experienced trainers will provide an insight on how to deal with these issues. Noticing what increases participants' involvement, excitement, and willingness to cooperate and what increases their confusion, disengagement, and feelings of wasting time will be very enlightening.

Timing

Many problems that new trainers experience involve losing control of time. When blocking out a program, the designer can estimate how long each portion should take; when the trainer is actually running the program, he or she can try to strike a balance between moving participants through the design and being flexible. Participants feel a sense of completion and of good organization if a pace is held that takes them through a progression of events. They do not like to feel that a program has become stuck. In fact, evaluations frequently indicate appreciation for trainers who deal effectively with participants who take the program off target.

It is important to decide how long a program needs to be and how many sessions are necessary or desired. Sometimes a program of a certain length is requested (for example, a one-day seminar or a two-hour staff meeting). At other times the decision about the optimum length for a program rests with a trainer and depends on a number of factors, including the following:

- What are the objectives for the program? How long must the program be to meet them? How much information needs to be included?
- What expectations do the participants have about program length and content depth? What do they need or want to know when the program is over?
- Is it the kind of program that lends itself to homework between sessions? Will participants benefit from a chance to practice skills between sessions and then discuss their experiences and receive coaching to sharpen these skills? (In a time-management workshop, for example, asking participants to keep a time log between sessions to provide data on how they actually spend their time can be more worthwhile than designing a longer, single-session program with similar content.)
- Do participants see the focus of the program as important enough to spend more than one session on it? Can they find time to attend all sessions, or will they be able to attend only some of them?

Designing a program of the right length can enhance the experience for participants. As Wlodkowski (1985) writes:

In general, the more lean the curriculum or program, the more learner attention it will gain. In this way, learners know that *all* the learning activities are valuable and build toward the competencies or knowledge they must exhibit. There is no busywork. (p. 39)

High-Risk Versus Low-Risk Programs

Another design question concerns how low or high the participants' risk factor should be. Depending on the goals, the objectives, the nature of the audience, and the participants' expectations, a program may be designed to have a low or a high risk factor. Of course, a program may also be designed to fit anywhere between the two extremes. Programs that ask for more self-assessment and self-disclosure generally are at the higher end of the risk continuum for most people. There are occasions when the training goals include building extensive trust and commitment (for example, a team-building workshop); and high-risk, intensive experiences can help to accomplish these goals. On the other hand, programs that are designed to impart information or build skills may not require much self-disclosure or risk taking.

Trainers need to be aware that a low risk for them might be a very high risk for the participants. Comfort and the risk level can be balanced to optimize learning. When designing a program that requires behaviors that might produce anxiety in some participants, the trainer can build the session to allow trust and comfort to grow first. This may be done by giving participants a chance to get their bearings, clarify their own goals and expectations, and feel connected to the group or to some individuals in the group.

Example: Creating an environment that encourages risk taking.

One goal in an assertive-communications workshop was to have participants practice behaviors and receive feedback. Individuals who elect to attend workshops on assertiveness often have difficulty talking in front of groups. In this instance the trainer designed a process that built comfort and trust, so participants willingly volunteered to role play. The program consisted of six sessions, and it led the participants through enough structured opportunities to create a feeling of intimacy and camaraderie. After a small-group session in which they used role-play scripts supplied by the trainer, they were ready to supply their own situations and work in the large group.

Even though these role plays were conducted in a controlled environment, feedback was allowed only on observed assertive behaviors. No negative feedback was allowed, and only the individuals involved in the role plays were allowed to publicly critique their own interactions.

Participants' discomfort with the tasks required of them can be quite obvious, or it can appear in a subtle manner. Therefore, it is important to pay attention to both verbal and nonverbal cues of increased tension and anxiety in participants, especially during activities requiring a great deal of participation and self-disclosure. Some discomfort can encourage learning, but too much can block it.

Testing the Design

The following guidelines will help the trainer to test the design:

- Try out every piece of a design that can be tried out.
- Fill out copies of the inventories and instruments before using them in a program.
- Ask colleagues and friends to fill them out and discuss what they learned.
- Preview all movies, slides, overhead transparencies, and so forth.
- Try out unfamiliar audiovisual equipment.
- Present lecturettes to colleagues and friends or, at the very least, in front of a mirror.

Practicing pieces of a design increases comfort when actually presenting them. A presenter's comfort and feelings of preparedness definitely are communicated to the participants. When the presenter is organized and self-confident, participants feel reassured that their time is being well spent and that the presenter has useful information for them. The more a presenter practices, the more likely it is that he or she will communicate comfort. Thorough preparation also allows a presenter more comfort and flexibility in dealing with the inevitable surprises that occur when training human beings.

Relationship of Design to Other Programs

It is important to think about an individual session or program in relation to other sessions or programs being presented. Each experience can build on others to optimize effect. If participants can see or experience some continuity of content, structure, or process across programs, learning can be increased and some resistance or barriers removed. For example, if all sessions begin with an opportunity to explore goals and expectations, participants can feel reasonably confident that questions about the goals and focus will be dealt with early in the training process. If participants are always told before a structured activity what kind of participation will be expected of them at the end, they will feel more in control of the risks they will be taking. For instance, if they are asked to complete an instrument and are told they will share their answers with the group, they can decide how self-revealing they want to be. The absence of surprises often increases participant comfort.

Using Humor

The use of humor in a training program is related to individual skill and comfort. Inappropriate humor can alienate an otherwise cooperative group of participants, whereas the skillful use of appropriate humor can increase participant comfort and even relieve tense situations. It is not a good idea to use humor if it does not come naturally. Humor can be useful at times, but it cannot take the place of enthusiasm and true involvement in building a group and establishing an energetic yet relaxed atmosphere.

Humor must be used only in ways that do not increase defensiveness or cause discomfort; it must either contribute to self-esteem or at least not affect anyone's self-esteem negatively. Sarcasm is especially risky; someone in the group might take it personally. On the other hand, a particularly relevant cartoon may add insight and humor to a packet of handouts. Similarly, a trainer's description of his or her own inept efforts at applying a concept can add a valuable human aspect to a presentation. Co-trainers have an opportunity to model effective, nonthreatening humor in their interactions with each other.

However, it is a good idea to be cautious and test the audience before jumping off the edge into silliness and theater-of-the-absurd antics. What is or is not funny changes for different audiences at different times. The political situation in an organization can make something that was funny one day deadly serious the next, and the addition of one specific individual to a group can change the meaning or impact of a joke. Trainers must be willing to laugh at themselves and general absurdities before they ask others to do the same.

CO-TRAINING VERSUS TRAINING ALONE

There are liabilities and assets associated with both co-training and training alone. On one hand, co-training offers opportunities for creativity of design, for feedback on training styles, for emergence of different perspectives, and to be rescued from tight spots. On the other hand, co-training can be more time consuming than conducting training alone and may be perceived as overkill by participants. Integrating different styles of communication and different perceptions of program focus can be very difficult.

Although it may be prudent to train alone if resources are limited, the trainer might want to seek some opportunities to co-train. This might be accomplished by volunteering to do a presentation with another trainer for a professional association or for a conference. Training alone can cause a loss of perspective about other ways to do things. Co-training provides a chance to be seen and critiqued and to receive feedback from respected colleagues, and having these opportunities is important for professional growth.

PROGRAM DOCUMENTATION

It is a good idea to establish procedures for documenting training programs. Writing down program goals, objectives, design components, and comments not only helps to clarify the planning phase, but also increases the likelihood of a smoothly run program. Documentation allows the program to be repeated with little confusion and offers a chance to critique and tailor the design.

Different systems of documentation are preferred for different trainers. For example, some like to keep a looseleaf notebook for each program presented. Such a notebook may include the following sections:

- An extensive outline of the program design, including a list of goals and objectives, notes for lecturettes, discussion questions, and so forth;
- Additional design ideas;
- Readings on the content topic;
- Planning notes;
- Administrative information and forms; and

- Evaluations with summaries of comments from program evaluation forms.

A one-page outline of the basic design for a program can indicate the amount of time to be spent on each section. The sheet can be used during a session to gauge whether a discussion should continue or whether the group should move to the next activity. The outline serves as an overview of the whole design and provides comfort, security, and flexibility.

Trainers use other organizational systems, of course, including index cards, computer-based outlines, and collections of newsprint sheets. It does not matter what actual procedures are used, but it is important that some are used.

The more explicit the documentation, the easier it is to update and repeat the program. Immediately after presenting a program, the trainer may make notes about what to do differently the next time. Before presenting the program again, the trainer can read the notes and the evaluation comments from the previous presentation.

HANDOUTS

Handouts can either add a great deal to a program or cause participants to feel overwhelmed by paper. They can add to the learning process, support the program goals, and allow people to participate more fully. Handouts can be used for the following purposes:

- To illustrate an important point more clearly or in a different way;
- To emphasize the importance of a concept;
- To help participants to see the relationship between the concepts presented and their work situation(s);
- To encourage self-assessment or increase self-awareness;
- To save participants from having to take copious notes; and
- To amuse in a relevant manner.

For example, a packet of handouts for a session on delegation might include an outline of the process of delegation, a list of suggestions for increasing the probability of success when delegating, a chart illustrating the relationship between authority and responsibility, a cartoon on dumping versus delegation, an instrument that explores the criteria that participants currently use to delegate work, some short cases used for discussion during the workshop, a reading on delegation, and a bibliography.

The practice of providing handouts can be abused, and the following guidelines are provided to help in avoiding pitfalls:

- Do not use handouts that are confusing and difficult to interpret.
- The amount of time a handout takes to interpret should be consistent with program priorities. Time is not used to good advantage by devising and using an overly complex handout supporting a simple concept.
- Do not use handouts just for the sake of giving people many sheets of paper to take away with them.
- Do not use handouts covered by copyrights without obtaining proper permission in advance.

Thought must be given to the way in which handouts will be distributed. The flow of a program can be seriously disrupted by constantly shuffling and distributing new handouts. On the other hand, if participants are given a packet of handouts, they are usually tempted to jump ahead, especially during less-stimulating sections of the program. A compromise would be to devise several small packets to be distributed at various times during the program. Strategic handouts (for example, self-assessment inventories) can be distributed just before they are to be used. If participants will receive a complete set of notes at the end, they may be told in advance so that they know they do not need to take notes during the sessions. The distribution of handouts should complement, rather than detract from, the intended flow of the program.

PROGRAM DESIGN AS
AN ORGANIZATIONAL INTERVENTION

The focus and content of programs can have much wider implications than the effect of increased participant knowledge. To ensure the continued existence of a training function, it is necessary to pay attention to how well the program goals, objectives, and content relate to organizational goals. Some organizations want only benign programs that do not really influence the way in which things are done; other organizations want programs that focus on useful content and further organizational goals. Trainers must be realistic and knowledgeable about what is preferred in their organizations.

Training programs, by their nature, bring people together in groups and often facilitate networking across departments. This activity can be seen as constructive in improving communications. It can also be seen as "stirring up the masses." Companies in which the chatting of four people at the water cooler is cause for concern about possible mutiny usually do not see training programs that foster discussions of problems in the work place as beneficial. The trainer must be aware of organizational goals and culture and must think about the impact of training.

Changes in behavior and increased self-esteem can be side effects of training programs. As Scherer (1984) writes:

> People are a gestalt, not isolated things. Thinking, feeling and doing are all interconnected. An activity aimed at one aspect will have profound effects on the other two. Be ready for unexpected effects from activities; remember that an event will kick off reactions in the whole person. (p. 65)

For example, participation in an assertiveness-training program can have the effect of empowering people to act differently in their work situations. Such behavioral change can cause conflicts and may be threatening to others. Some supervisors act punitively toward employees who become more assertive. In a healthy environment, feelings of empowerment and increased options of behavior can lead to increased self-esteem and personal satisfaction. These effects, in turn, can lead to increased motivation and job satisfaction. Participants in supervisory-skill workshops sometimes make comments such as "My manager should attend this workshop!" A participant's supervisor, manager, co-workers, and employees may be affected by changes in behavior, attitudes, or expectations that resulted from attending a program. As a catalyst for change—on an individual and organizational level—a trainer can prepare individuals and/or the organization for these possible side effects.

4

Choosing and Using
Training Methods

A trainer needs expertise in methods that can increase participant knowledge and skills as well as foster involvement and growth. Many learning structures or training methods exist and can be adapted or tailored for specific programs. Exposure to different ways of presenting information and creating learning experiences can increase a trainer's options in designing a new program.

Some training methods have enjoyed widespread use and are commonly known, such as lectures, demonstrations, discussions, and the use of audiovisual aids. Nevertheless, it is important to think periodically about how to re-energize these methods, improve their usefulness, and ensure their success in accomplishing program goals. Experienced trainers know about other training methods with which new trainers need to become familiar. These methods, which are used frequently in workshops and seminars and less often in traditional educational settings, include instruments, self-assessment activities, structured activities and experiential designs, original case studies, simulations, and games. New trainers may need an initial exposure to some of these methods, but all trainers need to work continually at learning new ways to apply them.

These methods or design options do not include all the technologies available to trainers. New training methods are continually being developed and polished, and old methods sometimes fade from popularity. For example, many trainers are rapidly trying to become facile with the possibilities of integrating computer technology into program design. This relatively new area of design currently ranges from software that allows individuals to learn content at their own pace in a question-and-answer format, to "whodunit" business cases presented in an interactive format for individuals or subgroups to unravel, to group activities for inclusion in a workshop. Books, workshops, and journal articles are being produced rapidly to help trainers to gain expertise in different aspects of using the computer in training.

Conversely, programmed learning is an example of a training method that does not enjoy the widespread use it once had. Although it can be useful at times and there are some good products on the market, many trainers now discount programmed learning as a viable tool.

It is important for trainers to increase their skills in using different training methods in order to design programs that communicate relevant content and provide variety for the participants. Because people have learning-style preferences, the use of a variety of methods can increase the likelihood of reaching more participants.

Variety of presentation in a program can significantly enhance participant learning, or it can distract and confuse. As Wlodkowski (1985) writes:

> Provide variety in personal presentation style, methods of instruction and learning materials. People tend to pay more attention to things that are changing than to things that are unchanging. However, variety simply for the sake of variety can be distracting. . . . Timing variety so that it can serve as a cue to important information or skills is probably one of the best ways to use it to the advantage of motivation and learning. How instructors use their bodies and voices can be a constant source of variety for their learners. This includes body movement, body language, voice (tone, pitch and pauses) and eye contact. There is also variety in methods of instruction and learning materials. . . . timely use of variety in materials or methods usually will stimulate adults. Also such changes prevent fatigue and often energize learners. As the old adage goes, "A change is as good as a rest." (p. 39)

Trainers need to be aware of their own preferences for presentation methods in order not to limit program structure by relying exclusively on personal favorites. Methods should be chosen because they will be most effective in building a fruitful learning experience. Participative and more passive styles may be interwoven to support program objectives and content and to reach a particular audience.

An effective training program is composed of a series of independent training methods that have been linked together as a result of giving forethought to order and purpose. In choosing training methods, it is helpful to think about a program as having a beginning, a middle, and an ending. Most training methods can be used in each phase, but attention to the differences in purpose of the phases can help in narrowing the choices for a given program.

This chapter focuses on some of the issues involved in the three phases of a program—the beginning, the middle, and the ending—and provides synopses and examples of some of the most popular training methods. Resources are listed at the end of the chapter to facilitate further study of these methods.

PHASES OF A PROGRAM

The Beginning

A program begins as soon as the first participant enters the room. Some participants arrive early, get settled, and start conversations; others like to use the time before a program begins to relax and catch their breath. In either case it is important to acknowledge people's arrival in some way, for example, by greeting them, by asking them to make name tags for themselves, or by offering them coffee. Talking casually with participants as they get settled can set an informal, conversational atmosphere for the program itself. At times it is useful to have a magazine article, a pertinent cartoon, or a brief questionnaire available for those who wish to jump into program content as they wait for others to arrive.

The design of a program can encourage participants to use all of their time in a beneficial way, including the time during which they are waiting for others to arrive. Because climate and expectations are built and influenced by every interaction that participants experience during a program, a well-conceived design can build realistic expectations, develop enthusiasm, and foster involvement.

Schindler-Rainman and Lippitt (1975) describe a "ragged" or staggered beginning as one technique to start workshops when all members are not yet present. They suggest designing an activity in which people begin working on a task that is central to the focus of the workshop and whose outcome will be used in the workshop itself. For example, in a time-management workshop, the trainer might post an announcement that reads as follows:

Welcome! While we wait for everyone to arrive for the workshop on time management, make yourself a name tag and take a copy of the handout entitled "Goals for This Workshop." Find yourself a seat and try to list your goals for this workshop. What would you like to learn and/or accomplish during the two sessions? When you have listed a few goals, sit down with another participant and spend some time talking about your goals. You might also discuss what you believe time management to be.

This process helps people to become involved in the workshop and its topic from the start; in addition, it models the effective use of time.

In opening a program, it is important to address the goals, objectives, and focus of that program as well as the expectations of the participants. Clarifying goals provides not only focus but also guidelines for measuring program success.

The opening of a workshop can be designed to help relieve the anxiety that accompanies most people's entrance into a new group and a new experience. Schein (1969) lists some concerns that arise and are dealt with in new groups. He writes that there is often a great deal of emotion attached to these concerns and that inattention to them may create problems in a group. Group members tend to deal with these issues in a number of ways; some ways are more productive and helpful than others. The group leader sets the tone for the way in which these issues are handled. The major concerns that Schein writes about involve the following issues:

1. **Identity.** How am I to function in this group? What roles do I want to play? What roles can I play?

2. **Control, power, and influence.** How much control, power, and influence do I have in this group? How much control, power, and influence do I want? Who are the other participants in this group, and what will I be in relation to them?

3. **Individual needs and group goals.** Will the group goals include my own needs? What are my needs in this group? What say do I have in establishing the group goals? What demands do the group goals make of me?

4. **Acceptance and intimacy.** Will the other group members like me? How close will the members be? What level of self-disclosure will be appropriate?

Although it is not easy to know when participants are dealing with these issues, it is a good idea to keep them in mind when deciding how to start a program. Methods that address them as early as possible can be chosen and used. In some programs it might make sense to let participants know that there are common issues in new groups. Ground rules for behavior in a program may be made explicit; participants may be alerted to what will be expected of them, both in preprogram literature and early in the program itself. For example, in programs with a personal-growth focus, such as assertive communications, participants may be asked to honor a ground rule of confidentiality. They may be told that they may talk with people outside the group about the design of the program and about their own feelings and experiences, but that they are not to talk about what other participants have shared regarding their lives, job situations, problems, and so forth. Then they may be asked if they have problems with the ground rule and if they will uphold it.

At the conclusion of programs in which this ground rule has been adopted, participants have often remarked or have written on evaluation sheets that they appreciated this confidentiality and that they were able to participate more fully and derive more from the experience because of the trust and supportive environment that were established. However, ground rules such as those concerning confidentiality will not work unless the trainer models adherence to them; participants should not be asked to uphold standards that the trainer intends to violate.

The Middle

The content and objectives of a program may be addressed in many ways with methods that support the content and allow participants to interact appropriately. One important aspect to consider is the flow of the design from one activity to the next.

If the program objectives involve teaching new skills, ample opportunity for practice should be provided. Learning can be increased when skills are practiced in the way in which they will be used on the job. Correct and incorrect examples of using a skill and the consequences of each will help participants to learn (Kelley, Orgel, & Baer, 1985).

The Ending

A well-designed program ending can increase transfer of learning to participants' work settings and provide data for evaluation of programs. An effective ending can provide an opportunity for participants to summarize their experience, to begin thinking of ways to apply what they have learned, and to give feedback on the program's effectiveness. (Chapter 5 deals specifically with the transfer of learning; Chapter 6 addresses evaluation.)

TRAINING METHODS

Many methods exist, or can be created, to involve participants in programs and to communicate information. The nature of such methods can vary from ones that are relatively low risk and demand little participant involvement to ones whose success is dependent on the ability of participants to become involved and highly committed to the process.

The methods summarized in this chapter are presented in order of increasing participant involvement. Each summary includes a description of the method, ideas about when to use it, and concerns and issues to be considered in choosing it. Some of the summaries also include actual examples of the kinds of handouts that can be designed to support those methods. The methods covered are some of the more widely used: lectures/lecturettes; demonstrations; discussions; audiovisual aids; case studies; self-assessment instruments and activities; and structured experiences, including simulations and games.

At the end of this chapter is a list of resources for training methods. Before reproducing activities or handouts, the trainer should always check the copyright requirements of the volume and obtain permission if necessary. Some publishers encourage the use of designs and only require acknowledgment of the source; other publishers require that copies be purchased from them. There are laws protecting copyright, and an organization can be held responsible if a trainer breaks them.

Lectures/Lecturettes

Lectures are used to explain concepts and issues. They can be especially effective in communicating a lot of information in a short time to a large group, particularly when more participative methods might be too time consuming. Because lectures are a passive vehicle, it is often a good idea to integrate them into a program with strategies that require people to be active learners.

Lecturettes are short presentations that can be given when a concept needs clarification or the participants will benefit from some conceptual input. They allow a trainer to present information immediately before or after an activity in order to raise or clarify an issue or concept.

Example: Using a lecturette.

A workshop on office communications included an activity in which participants worked in subgroups to experiment with different styles of communication. Before introducing the activity, the trainer talked about when to use different listening techniques and the benefits of each. To increase participant learning, he also provided handouts that presented the key concepts of the lecturette.

The information in a lecturette can come from readings done in the research phase of the design process. Current journal articles are excellent sources of new concepts and trends in organizational issues. Some volumes on program design contain information to help trainers in creating lecturettes.

The more familiar a trainer becomes with a content area, the easier it is to integrate relevant lecturettes into a workshop. Lecturettes have the greatest impact when presented at the time that a concept has been discovered or brought out in a group. Consequently, the trainer needs to be not only prepared to present but also flexible about the timing of lecturettes.

Demonstrations

Demonstrations of skills or concepts can be effective additions to lectures or substitutions for them. Providing opportunities for participants to see what is being described can increase audience participation in terms of questions, discussions, and observations.

Demonstrations have traditionally been used for technical skill training on topics ranging from how to operate a lathe to how to make an omelet.

The trainer should accept the fact that a demonstration may turn out differently than expected. We all know about chemistry demonstrations that have literally blown up; that kind of problem is not likely to happen in a workshop, but things can "go wrong." However, any outcome can be used to help participants to question, discuss, and clarify concepts that are relevant to a program's objectives. The trainer needs to remain nondefensive and open to what can be learned from any experience.

A technique that is slightly less exciting than the live demonstration but still valuable is to prerecord a demonstration on videotape and then use it to emphasize points or to generate discussion. One real advantage to this method is that the trainer may accompany the presentation with observations and comments because the videotape may be started, stopped, played, and replayed.

Example: Using a videotaped demonstration.

In a communications workshop, a series of prerecorded, staged office interactions between employees and their supervisors were used to focus on nonverbal behavior. The interactions were played initially without sound, and participants were asked to discuss what they thought was happening on the basis of the nonverbal behaviors exhibited. Then the videotapes were replayed with sound. Through this technique the participants became more keenly aware of the effects of nonverbal behavior on communication than they would have if a lecture alone had been provided.

Discussions

Group discussions can be either exciting and lively or uncomfortable and deadly. Historically, learning situations have consisted of lectures and, if participation was allowed, total-group discussions. Even though most people educated in the United States have experience with these two learning situations, it does not mean that they feel comfortable with them or know how to benefit from them. Lecturettes and total-group discussions should not be used as fillers; instead, they should be used when they will contribute to the learning process or goals.

Because fear of speaking in front of a group is widespread, it is important to build comfort in small steps in order to encourage people to participate. Most people will participate in subgroup discussions if they are given explicit directions for discussion content and if the content is intrinsically linked to their experience.

Example: Using participants' experience to build comfort and encourage discussion.

In a program designed for new supervisors, the first session focused on defining and clarifying the characteristics of effective supervision. Participants were asked to assemble into subgroups of four or five and to discuss their best and worst supervisors. The participants were asked not to refer to these individuals by name but to talk about what they did that caused their classification as "best" and "worst." All of the participants had unique experiences to contribute, and animated discussions ensued. When the total group was reconvened, a list of characteristics of effective supervision was created from the material generated in the subgroup discussions.

One way to develop total-group discussions is to build them from previous subgroup discussions. For example, participants may be asked to report specific types of information from their subgroups, or they may be asked to complete a task in subgroups and report the outcome. Relevant questions from the trainer can then spark a lively total-group discussion:

1. What similarities and differences emerged in your subgroups?
2. What trends emerged during your subgroup discussions? Were certain thoughts or ideas repeated and agreed to by several members?
3. What surprises emerged in your discussions?
4. Which subgroups haven't we heard from? What things do you have to add?

If subgroups have been asked to brainstorm about a case or generate solutions to a problem, often they are asked to share their responses in the total group. Because it can be incredibly boring to listen to several groups relate similar answers at great length, it is wise to give specific instructions to generate a more interesting total-group discussion. Following are three different approaches to providing such instructions (Schindler-Rainman & Lippitt, 1975):

1. Each subgroup may be asked to choose its three favorite ideas and to report one of these three. After all subgroups have reported, the trainer may elicit any remaining ideas that have not already been mentioned.

2. Each subgroup may be asked to report only one or two especially good ideas.

3. The subgroups may be asked to post newsprint lists of all their ideas. Then the trainer may ask each participant to choose and put a check mark next to each of three favorite ideas from each list. When everyone finishes, the total group may be reconvened to discuss the ideas that received the greatest numbers of check marks and what they particularly liked about those ideas. Implications of the most popular choices and the lack of votes for other ideas may be explored.

Total-group discussions can be especially useful when it is important to accomplish the following goals:

- To explore the same concepts at the same time;
- To hear the same ideas;
- To generate a wide variety of ideas, opinions, and viewpoints;
- To wrap up a segment of a program or a concept and to provide a summary;
- To create a change in mood;
- To give participants an opportunity to ask questions, check perceptions, and explore together as a group; and
- To build total-group unity and a sense of team.

Good total-group discussions do not just happen. Either the trainer must build a climate that allows participants to feel comfortable enough to participate, or the topic must be so compelling that they cannot bear to be quiet. It is important to structure the situation so that as many individuals as possible can participate as quickly as possible. People who speak early in a group situation often continue to make contributions; when people wait a long time before speaking, sometimes they become self-conscious and censor their own contributions. Open-ended, carefully worded questions from the trainer can help to generate individual contributions and, consequently, a good total-group discussion. When a group reaches its own conclusions and voices them, the resulting learning experience is more powerful than when the same statements are made by the presenter.

Audiovisual Presentations

The use of films, slide-and-tape shows, overhead projectors, video-tapes, and audiotapes can add variety to a workshop. These media may be used instead of a lecture to add content to a program, or they may be used to present visual or audio case studies. As Faris (1984) writes:

> A well selected film can vary the pace of the training day, capture attention, provide comic relief, offer entertainment, drive home a point, illustrate concepts that cannot be readily observed, provide the opportunity to learn from a recognized expert and so on. But a film can never substitute for an instructor. A film may be a useful tool, but only the instructor can tie film content to learning objectives. (p. 108)

Commercial products exist in such abundance that it can seem overwhelming to contemplate finding the best item to use. Several techniques can help:

1. *Save all catalogs and brochures that arrive in the mail.* They will come in handy when it is time to design a specific program. When that time arrives, try to look through them with an eye toward only the topic of interest.

2. *Preview all audiovisuals before using them.* In reality they are often not exactly as they are described in catalogs and brochures. Keep good critical notes on each product and its content. Invite members of the potential audience to preview and critique each film being considered. If a film is particularly good but the setting is radically different from the one in which the participants function, develop ways to link the two settings so that the participants can relate to the film more easily.

There are many ways to preview audiovisual products. In larger cities, there are often preview resource services that represent several audiovisual companies. Ask such services to find products to preview on a specific topic, and go to their facilities to preview them. These companies earn their profits from rentals and from purchases made after previews; therefore, the actual previewing is free. Sometimes these services allow products to be borrowed so that organizational decision makers can have an opportunity to preview and evaluate. Using this approach can save considerable money, time, and coordination effort.

Previews set up through film companies are usually costly and take several weeks to accomplish. Occasionally, a film company will send an offer for free previews of new products. Sometimes companies offer screening days for a nominal fee to let prospective clients view many films at once. This method of previewing can be useful but absolutely exhausting; after viewing three or four films in succession, anyone can find it difficult to judge appropriateness and relevance. Conferences provide another opportunity to view popular products; often there are screening rooms showing a variety of titles. Another alternative is to ask other trainers which products they have had success with and then preview them. In addition, current journals sometimes contain reviews of new products.

3. ***Become completely familiar with and test audiovisual equipment before using it.*** Even if a projector has been used earlier the same day, for example, it could need a new bulb or an extension cord if it is to be used in a different room.

4. ***When judging whether to use an audiovisual product, analyze whether it is appropriate for the specific situation.*** Ask the following questions:

- What will the product add to the program?
- Will participants be able to relate to the product, to its setting, to its characters, and to the problems or ideas presented?
- Is it an appropriate length for the concepts portrayed? Is it too long and repetitive? Is it too short and simplistic?
- Is it appropriate for the intellectual level of the participants, or is it patronizing and condescending?
- Does it present information in novel or particularly intriguing ways?
- Is it sexist, racist, or offensive in some other way? For example, does it portray only white male managers, female secretaries, or minority-group members in the performance of menial tasks?
- Will it provide useful variety?
- Will it contribute new perspectives?
- Will it generate a good discussion?

Integration of an Audiovisual Presentation

Much of the success of using an audiovisual presentation depends on how it is integrated into a program. Some products generate excellent discussions, while others require help from the trainer to enable participants to learn from them. Some films are so powerful that afterward participants need some time to digest their feelings and reactions before discussing them in the total group; on such occasions they may be asked to work alone on a structured writing exercise or to work in small subgroups on answers to specific questions. Other films generate a lively exchange of opinions, while still others lead to thoughtful explorations of a concept or a case.

It is helpful to think carefully about how to introduce the presentation and to prepare questions to generate discussions. As Faris (1984) suggests:

> Provide a synopsis of the film. Don't be afraid to be critical, but do not apologize for it. Merely because it is old does not mean that it is bad. Tell the trainees the purpose of the film, the general order it follows, and its strengths and weaknesses. Explain the specific things you want the viewers to notice. This sets expectations, helps viewers pay attention and provides an opportunity for self-administered reinforcements. (p. 109)

Creating Versus Hiring Professionals to Create

Many trainers prefer to develop their own videotapes, audiotapes, slides, and overhead transparencies. Although the quality of these products is usually not as high as that of ones produced professionally, their appeal often lies in the relevance of the topics and concepts raised. Knowing a product is "home grown" sometimes allows participants to forgive technical defects and to focus more quickly on the issues raised. A video interaction between an employee and a supervisor that lasts three or four minutes can easily generate twenty minutes of discussion.

Short video or audio interactions may be used in much the same way as short case studies. Often a formal script is unnecessary and actually hinders the success of the tape; ad-lib lines can subsequently give rise to more effective discussions of the situation, what led up to it, and what could have been said instead. The beauty of creating audiotapes or videotapes is the relative simplicity of the technology. Cameras can be rented or borrowed, and mistakes can be corrected with little cost.

There are times when it is worth the expense to hire professionals to produce an audiovisual product that is free of surprises and extremely attractive, for example when the product is to be presented to a prospective client or to senior management. Also, when an audiovisual product will be used very frequently, for example as part of an orientation for new employees, the expense of using outside professionals may be justified. A slide-and-tape show or videotape can create the same enthusiasm and ambiance several hundred times; no presenter can make the same claim.

Case Studies

Case studies involve descriptions of unresolved situations for group discussion and generation of solutions. Cases can be lengthy and formal, or they can be extremely brief descriptions of single incidents. They can be about imaginary companies, situations, and people; or they can be descriptions of real problems, facts, and decisions. They can be about situations that are presently happening and really are unresolved, or they can be historical with outcome data to be discussed. Formal cases are used in many business courses and can be reviewed and purchased through several sources. Because of their length and complexity, these kinds of cases are usually given to participants to read before a session.

Short case studies created from data received during needs assessment or planning discussions can be quite effective. Because they can be read quickly and usually generate immediate reactions, they may be distributed and used during a session. A trainer can prepare and use a series of such case studies focused on the particular content of a program.

Example: Cases used in program for supervisors on dealing with personnel problems.

Case 1: Dorothy
Dorothy has worked in your office for about six months. She told you that she transferred from another area of the company because the work was not challenging and she was bored. Her

job in your area is somewhat complex, and you have tried to be quite patient with the number of mistakes she makes. Whenever you catch an error, you try to explain to her what the problem is and how to avoid it in the future. Dorothy is always very cooperative when you give her this feedback; she nods her head and says that she understands and that she has no questions. Unfortunately, your efforts to help her correct her errors do not seem to be having the desired result; she still makes the same or very similar mistakes.

The last time you talked with Dorothy, you asked her if she was happy with her job and if she thought she was getting a good grasp of it. She said that she loved working in this office and that she was sure she could do the job.

You just received a call from your supervisor complaining about a memo with incorrect information. Dorothy wrote the memo and mailed it to a number of people.

What options do you have? What do you decide to do?

Case 2: Gregory and Cynthia

You are an administrator in a laboratory, and you supervise eight people. Gregory and Cynthia, two of the research assistants who work for you, have never gotten along. Individually they do their work adequately; and, as long as they do not have to interact much, things get done. You generally avoid pairing them on projects so that you do not have to end up dealing with their arguments.

One day another staff member comes into your office and says, "I've had it! Gregory and Cynthia are driving me crazy. I can't spend another day waiting for the caustic remarks to fly past, and I'm not the only one who's fed up with those two." What are your options? How do you respond?

Andrews and Noel (1986) describe living case studies in the following way:

Instead of studying something that happened in the past, participants work on a major unresolved challenge facing the company. . . .

The living case is based on a current problem or management decision facing an organization. It is not a single document but a collection of data, much like that available to managers, to sort through and organize. (p. 28)

Finding a case study that exactly fits the bill is difficult. Therefore, it often makes sense to write a case that is especially relevant to the participants. Boyd (undated) suggests a six-step process for writing such cases:

1. Define the principles you are trying to bring a group to understand.
2. Establish a situation that illustrates the principle.
3. Develop the symptoms.
4. Develop the characters.
5. Write the case.
6. Conclude with questions. (pp. 95-96)

Sometimes people are intimidated by the notion of writing cases because they are convinced that their cases must be perfect. In actuality, cases are useful because they are incomplete segments of working life; even bad cases can generate wonderful discussions about how working in an organization is quite different from what has been portrayed in the case. The trainer needs to be prepared to allow appropriate discussions to develop even if they are not what was anticipated, but should not allow inappropriate critiques (for example, comments about the grammar used in a case) to consume a lot of group time. A good approach is to simply acknowledge that a case is not meant to win a Nobel Prize for literature, to encourage useful discussion instead, and to try not to be defensive about how a case is interpreted.

Discussions of case studies may occur in small or large subgroups and/or in the total group.

Self-Assessment Activities and Instruments

There are numerous activities and instruments with origins in psychology, research studies, sociological studies, and the human relations field. Through these mechanisms participants can learn about and compare their styles, attitudes, beliefs, values, and preferences with those of others in their field or elsewhere; develop an understanding of a model or concept and a basis for discussing it; and learn about how they see the world. There are also collections of research instruments, indexed by various topics, for use in program design. If the purpose of using an instrument is to raise awareness and connection to a field of research is less important, an original instrument may be designed and may be as complex or as simple as is necessary.

Example: Using an original self-assessment instrument.

Participants in an assertive-communications workshop may be asked to complete the following sentences in order to identify some of their history and styles of dealing with assertiveness:

1. *Right now I feel...*
2. *I have least trouble being assertive with...*
3. *I have most trouble being assertive with...*
4. *The positive consequences of being assertive are...*
5. *The negative consequences of being assertive are...*
6. *When I want something but don't want to ask for it, I...*
7. *Aggression...*
8. *When I want to speak up, my body...*
9. *If I say "no,"...*
10. *Expressing a need to someone else is...*
11. *When someone asks me to do something I don't want to do, I...*
12. *When I have to ask someone to do something, I...*

When two individuals share their sentence completions, the activity is called a "dyadic encounter" (Pfeiffer & Jones, 1969). Reading examples of these activities can be useful in creating new ones, and looking through collections of instruments is one way to become familiar with the many formats and styles that are available.

No matter what kind of activity or instrument is chosen, it is important to integrate it into the training design appropriately, introduce it properly, and clarify how the information generated will be used. Participants should be told in advance how much they will be asked to share with fellow subgroup members or in the total group; for example, before completing an instrument, they should be told whether their scores will be recorded publicly and compared with those of other participants.

Some instruments result in a computed score. Before using such an instrument, the trainer needs to know how to interpret these scores and how to explain them. Participants become emotionally involved in scores, and it is important not to raise their defensiveness or diminish their self-esteem. Debriefing is a crucial step in the use of both scored instruments and activities used for self-assessment; participants need time to understand the meaning of the instrument or activity, to think about it in a realistic framework, and to share and deal with any feelings and reactions that they may have. An instrument or activity that is not well integrated into the design can result in more problems than benefits; for example, without appropriate debriefing, participants may be extremely reluctant to move on to another part of a program.

Instead of completing a written instrument, participants may be asked to use felt-tipped markers, crayons, magazine pictures, and so forth to create images of themselves. With specific instructions, they can generate and order information in ways that can help them to identify trends or styles in their lives. Again, they need to know how they will be asked to use the information generated. Sometimes they may be asked to share their creations; at other times they may be asked only to share the trends that they have discovered. When they have completed such an activity, it is usually helpful to provide questions for them to answer to help them integrate the information generated.

Example: Using a self-assessment activity and providing processing questions.

Participants in a workshop on career choices were asked to use crayons, markers, magazine pictures, and glue to create time lines indicating major educational, personal, and job-related experiences since they left high school. The following time-line analysis form was used to help them to clarify trends in their completed time lines:

Time-Line Analysis

1. *If you could say only three things about your time line, what would you say?*
2. *Where were there turning points? Where were there missed opportunities?*
3. *Describe those situations in which you were learning the most. . . learning the least.*
4. *Describe those situations in which you were the happiest. . . least happy. Do you see any patterns?*

Structured Experiences

Structured experiences are designed so that members of groups can learn about some content through participation in a process. For example, instead of learning about styles of decision making by listening to a lecture, participants may be asked to make a series of decisions and then reflect on and share the processes that they used. The power of a structured experience comes from the degree of personal involvement on the part of the participants and from the trainer's ability to help the participants understand and learn from what happened. A well-designed structured experience that is used at an appropriate point in a workshop can be extremely effective in making a concept more concrete and can result in an enormous payoff in terms of increased awareness and perceived relevance.

Structured experiences can be quite simple and short, or they can be extremely complex and require a lot of setup and time. It is important to select or design experiences that are closely tied to the objectives of a program. They should not be more time consuming, either in setup or presentation, than is necessary. It is easy to be seduced by a clever design even if it will not increase learning.

Often designs can be adapted to suit the program objectives. As Pfeiffer (1985) writes:

> Any given activity may be equally appropriate in a leadership-development design or in a session focusing on team development, but because the goals of the two events may be significantly different, the processing of the data generated by the structured experience will be decidedly different. For example, in a structured experience that we have used from time to time in laboratories, the facilitator distributes materials and gives the group members the task of organizing themselves to construct a checkerboard. In a basic human relations laboratory, the behavioral and feeling data that are generated by such an experience probably would be processed in a T-group meeting in which people would focus on their own emerging awareness and on their feeings and reactions to other people's behavior. They would be given feedback of a very personal nature about the effects of the process and the effects of one another's behavior. In a leadership-development laboratory, the same event might be processed in terms of leadership styles that emerged during the event, styles of influence, roles people played, and decision-making procedures. There also might be an attempt to process the data in terms of a theory of leadership.

Structured experiences generate and focus data toward particular learnings, but the major skill in their use is in adapting them to the particular learning needs of the participants and in assisting participants in processing and integrating data that are generated by their use. (pp. 18-19)

Simulations and games are large-scale structured experiences. They provide an opportunity for the whole group to be involved in an activity that will allow a great deal of interaction and data generation. They are usually complex and time consuming to set up, to become familiar with in terms of process and possible outcomes, and to conduct. They also require a high degree of skill in helping participants to debrief, integrate the learnings, and deal with the feelings that were raised.

In deciding whether to use a game or simulation, the trainer should determine whether the outcome justifies the time, effort, and emotional investment usually required. If living through an experience will crystallize learning and the strength of that learning is very important, using a simulation or game can be a good idea. For example, some of the simulations that teach the impact of racism or other "isms" can be very powerful and useful in helping people to come to terms with themselves. For example, simulations that allow participants to run companies briefly allow for a type of learning that even case studies will not convey. Before using a simulation or game, the trainer should find out who else uses it, arrange to participate in it, and ask what outcomes can be expected and what to watch for to assist participants in gaining the most from the experience.

Listed at the end of this chapter are a number of resources for structured experiences. Flipping through volumes of designs is useful in terms of priming one's own creativity; so is thinking about personal or others' experiences that have crystallized a concept, cleared up confusion, or helped to resolve a problem. The trainer should try to imagine ways to create similar opportunities for clarification in workshops.

RESOURCES

Publishers

Sources of training designs, instruments, cases, structured experiences, games, simulations, and books on training:

Addison-Wesley Publishing Co., Inc.
Jacob Way
Reading, MA 01867

American Management Association
135 West 50th Street
New York, NY 10020

Goodmeasure, Inc.
330 Broadway
P.O. Box 3004
Cambridge, MA 02139

Harvard Business School
Intercollegiate Case Clearing House
Soldier's Field
Boston, MA 02163

John Wiley and Sons, Inc.
605 Third Avenue
New York, NY 10158

Jossey-Bass, Inc.
433 California Street
Suite 1000
San Francisco, CA 94104

Lakewood Publications, Inc.
Lakewood Building
50 South Ninth Street
Minneapolis, MN 55402

McGraw-Hill
674 Via de la Valle
Solana Beach, CA 92075

Organization Design and Development
101 Bryn Mawr Avenue
Suite 310
Bryn Mawr, PA 19010

Ten Speed Press
P.O. Box 7123 EET
900 Modoc Street
Berkeley, CA 94707

University Associates, Inc.
8517 Production Avenue
San Diego, CA 92121

Journals

Sources of discussions of issues and trends, program-design ideas, outcomes of research studies, conceptual models, and content for lecturettes:

Personnel Journal
245 Fischer Avenue B-2
Costa Mesa, CA 92626

Training and Development Journal
American Society for Training and Development
1630 Duke Street
Box 1443
Alexandria, VA 22313

Training: The Magazine of Human Resources Development
Lakewood Publications, Inc.
Lakewood Building
50 South Ninth Street
Minneapolis, MN 55402

Audiovisual Resources

Sources of films, videotapes, audiotapes, and slide-and-tape presentations:

Advantage Media, Inc.
4121 Redwood Avenue
Los Angeles, CA 90066

AMA Film/Video
American Management Association
85 Main Street
Watertown, MA 02172

BNA Communications, Inc.
The Bureau of National Affairs, Inc.
9439 Key West Avenue
Rockville, MD 20850

Barr Films
3490 East Foothill Boulevard
P.O. Box 5667
Pasadena, CA 91107

The Cally Curtis Company
111 North Las Palmas Avenue
Hollywood, CA 90038

CRM/McGraw-Hill Films
P.O. Box 641
Del Mar, CA 92014-9988

Clark Communications, Inc.
Suite 907
Fox Plaza
1390 Market Street
San Francisco, CA 94102

5

Increasing Transfer of Learning

The value of many programs is judged by the participants' ability to apply their new learnings and skills in the day-to-day activities of their jobs. Research and experience have shown that there are particular methods for increasing the likelihood that participants will be able to apply workshop learnings, and the trainer should try to integrate these methods into workshop design. It is not enough to conduct needs assessments and ensure that content areas are relevant to participants; in addition, programs must be designed to encourage the application of learning.

RATIONALE AND OBJECTIVES

The judgment of training programs on the basis of whether participants are subsequently more effective in their jobs constitutes a fair and reasonable measure of success. If participants are helped to be more efficient, more effective, or more satisfied, productivity will generally improve and management support will often increase. Conversely, as Michalak and Yager (1979) state, managers have the right to question the value of training if employees are not using the skills and concepts taught. Michalak and Yager conducted a study on the maintenance of behavior in an industrial setting involving six different maintenance methods used in conjunction with a supervisory-skills program. The outcome of the study supported the importance of using particular methods to transfer and maintain workshop learning:

> The results showed an almost perfect correlation between the quantity and quality of the maintenance of behavior efforts and the results obtained in each department. In those departments where the managers put time and effort into maintaining the behavior learned by their supervisors, the beneficial results of the

training program were still in force 6 and 12 months later. In those departments where less attention was given to the maintenance portion of the program, the positive effects of the training had all but disappeared 6 to 12 months later. (p. 120)

Efforts to increase transfer of learning are aimed at producing attachments or building linkages (Nadler, 1976c) that enable participants to associate the concepts and skills taught with the actual work and problems that they face in their jobs. Such linkages can be produced or encouraged through many techniques, but they are sometimes blocked by obstacles existing in the work environment.

WORK ENVIRONMENT

Certain characteristics of the work environment either support or obstruct the transfer and maintenance of learning. Trost (1985, p. 78) notes, ". . . new behaviors often feel awkward and uncomfortable. Without active support and encouragement it is easy to slip back into old, familiar patterns before the new skills become established habits." He suggests that trainers need to become aware of the jargon, hot topics, and rumors existing in the participants' home organizations; he cautions (p. 78) that "Knowing what the sore spots are and what to avoid saying can be just as important as knowing what to say."

Other writers (Robinson & Robinson, 1985; Trapnell, 1984) support the notion of conducting environmental evaluations to assess attitudes and barriers concerning training in organizations. Robinson and Robinson delineate three types of barriers to skill transfer: those the learner brings to the situation, those the learner's immediate supervisor creates, and those within the organization. They suggest that thorough knowledge of the barriers that exist enables the trainer to work with supervisors and management to remove or reduce them prior to a training effort. They also acknowledge environmental enhancers, that is, those forces in an organization that encourage and support transfer and maintenance of learning.

METHODS TO ENCOURAGE TRANSFER AND MAINTENANCE OF LEARNING

The methods commonly used to encourage transfer and maintenance of learning are of four basic types:

1. Preparing a more receptive on-the-job environment by directly involving supervisors and managers in the program;
2. Providing workshop opportunities to apply concepts and practice skills so that participants can integrate workshop learnings more closely with their job situations;
3. Planning specific actions to be taken after the workshop ends; and
4. Planning and conducting follow-up activities and/or meetings.

Involving Supervisors and Managers

Many techniques that increase on-the-job receptiveness and support for training are based on involvement of the participants' supervisors and managers. Michalak and Yager (1979) state:

> The single most important factor in maintaining the behavior of trainees once they return to their jobs is whether or not there is any positive reinforcement coming from the managers of the trainees. Positive reinforcement coming from immediate supervisors is the most powerful maintenance system. (p. 125)

Managers and supervisors can be involved in supporting a training effort before, during, and after the actual event. The groundwork for transfer and maintenance of learning can be laid before a program begins. The trainer can involve managers in the needs-assessment process in order to learn their perceptions and incorporate their wishes for program outcome. Both managers and potential participants can shed light on specific skills and concepts to be included in program content. For some programs, managers can be involved in participant selection; they can be asked to choose participants who will use the skills to be taught and to explain to those participants why they were chosen and what is expected of them.

The more a participant and a supervisor discuss the purpose and anticipated outcomes of a training effort, the more likely the success of the program. Discussing the focus and objectives before a program will aid in identifying environmental supports and barriers and in finding ways to enhance supports and remove or reduce obstacles.

Managerial effort to remove or reduce obstacles to transfer and maintenance of learning is one of the most effective interventions that can be used. Michalak and Yager (1979) stress how important it is for managers to let participants know about their efforts to remove obstacles so that changes are seen as part of the training effort rather than as chance occurrences.

Trost (1985) suggests that trainers invest time in working directly with participants' managers prior to the program. He states that a training session for the managers could prepare them to discuss program outcome with their employees, to delineate program content, and to clarify their role in the transfer and maintenance of learning.

There are several ways for managers to be involved during the training program. They can participate in a trial run of the program so that they know what is covered and how it can apply. They can also participate in part of the actual program with trainees. Michalak and Yager (1979) suggest that after experiencing part of a program, managers should be given an opportunity to discuss their roles in maintaining behavior and the specific activities that they will undertake to fulfill those roles.

Example: Training managers first.

Robert, a vice president of a large architectural firm, wanted to increase staff awareness of the importance of providing good customer service. He was interested in providing training, particularly for the clerical staff, but he wanted the professional staff to be involved as well. Although he did not want to offend the members of the professional staff by implying that they too needed training in customer service, he wanted their awareness and concern to be raised.

When Robert contacted Terry, the training director, Terry suggested that training be planned for the clerical staff but that a pilot session of the program be presented to members of the professional staff; in this way the professionals could be asked to evaluate the potential effectiveness of the program and to suggest changes, and at the same time they could be trained in the program content. Robert agreed to this approach. The pilot was conducted, and time was included at the end of the program for a discussion of suggested changes and identification of obstacles to the program's success. The members of the professional staff became involved in very useful discussions about providing better customer service and what they did to promote or inhibit it.

The pilot, therefore, accomplished three goals: (1) it heightened the professional staff's awareness about improving the customer-service orientation of the company; (2) it increased the likelihood of program success through the identification and removal of obstacles; and (3) it provided an informed critique of the program before company-wide implementation began.

While a program is actually being conducted, managers may be actively involved in the process. Stovall (1975) suggests that participants be encouraged to set up appointments to discuss with their supervisors what they are learning. Kelley, Orgel, and Baer (1985) write about encouraging participants to document their successes in applying their learnings and to report these efforts to their supervisors.

Supervisory involvement is a powerful design component and should not be attempted without the supervisors' thorough knowledge and agreement. Designs that request supervisors to meet with participants, provide performance feedback on a form, or attend briefings on a program require commitments of the supervisors' time. Even those who believe in the concept of training may be rightfully annoyed if they agree to an employee's attending a training session without prior knowledge that the commitment involves their own time as well. The trainer must obtain informed consent and voluntary involvement; otherwise, attempts to increase transfer of learning may fail.

Providing Opportunities to Apply Concepts and Practice Skills

The design of a program can provide many opportunities for participants to make connections between the concepts and skills taught and their day-to-day jobs. At the start of a program, participants may be asked to share their expectations and goals in order to allow the trainer to tailor the program. Trost (1985) suggests that participants be asked the following questions:

What 2 or 3 things do you most want to learn from this training? When we're done and you look back on the training, what will you have learned that will make you say it was well worth the time? What will you be doing differently as a result of this training? (p. 79)

Participants who write their objectives and share them with the group are often more committed to them. With this information a trainer can let participants know which needs realistically cannot be met by the program and can also tailor the program to concentrate on what is most relevant to the participants.

The program design can include activities—such as role plays and case studies—that give participants opportunities to apply concepts, solve problems, and practice skills. Kelley, Orgel, and Baer (1985) point out that the more similarities that exist between practice situations and real work situations, the easier it is to transfer learning. They caution that trainers should not attempt to include too many skills in a program and that adequate practice time be allowed with one skill before a new skill is introduced. They also suggest that both correct and incorrect examples be supplied and that participants be asked to correct the problems and discuss the consequences.

Trost (1985) and Newstrom (1975) emphasize the importance of giving feedback to participants on their efforts to practice new skills. The opportunity to have successful experiences in practicing a new skill can help in building confidence and enabling participants to try that skill on the job (Michalak & Yager, 1979).

The practice of skills can be supported further by requiring participants to document their attempts to apply skills on the job. Trost (1985) suggests having participants join with partners for reinforcement and practice between sessions of a program. In addition, to help participants clarify and solidify their learnings, Michalak and Yager (1979) suggest asking them to spend a few minutes at the end of a session recording the more relevant or important ideas of that session.

During a session the trainer should be very aware of his or her role in modeling the concepts being presented. As Trost (1985) points out, a trainer in a communication workshop should model good communication skills. Behavior that models the concepts being taught not only provides useful examples but also builds the trainer's credibility.

Example: Using trainer behavior as a role model.

Jane, a trainer in a workshop on assertive communications, asked each participant to share one goal for the workshop. When they had finished, Jane asked them to comment on their own behavior in terms of being assertive. She asked them to discuss how they had felt physically prior to, during, and after the goal sharing. She also asked if they had acted typically or atypically by volunteering to talk early in the process, waiting to talk, or trying not to talk at all.

After a discussion of their behavior, Jane instructed them to focus on her own behavior as a listener. She asked what she had done that encouraged their participation and what behaviors, statements, and actions had made her more or less effective as a listener.

The goal-sharing activity had, therefore, accomplished several purposes: (1) it provided information on some of the participants' goals; (2) it provided an opportunity for all members to talk in a group and then process their own participation; (3) it provided examples of effective listening; and (4) it established a norm of critically and constructively examining participant and trainer behavior for examples of effective communication.

Action Planning

The program design may include an opportunity for participants to plan how they will put their learnings to use on the job. They need to think about the changes they will attempt, whom they can depend on for support, and how they can increase the probability of their success. Trost (1985) reports that action plans tend to work best if participants are limited in their choice to no more than three objectives, are asked to assess the difficulties that they might encounter in implementing their plans, and are asked to share their plans with the total group.

Although the process of developing and using an action plan is time consuming, it ensures continued commitment, especially if the plan is realistic, includes the intention to try new skills, and is made public. Michalak and Yager (1979) suggest initiating the action-planning process by asking participants three questions at the end of a training program:

1. What have you learned about the topic of this program?
2. What have you learned about yourself?
3. How will your learnings affect your job?

They continue by stating that the trainer can help participants to clarify their action plans by asking questions about what new thoughts or ideas have been generated by the training, what the participants want to do differently, what help is needed from others, and what obstacles need to be overcome. Marx (1986) states that to assist participants in determining how, where, and from whom support will be needed, the trainer should ask each participant to identify the work situation that poses the greatest threat to long-term skill retention. He also suggests asking each participant to predict the circumstances of his or her first lapse in using a new behavior in order to prevent the occurrence of such a lapse. The use of an action-planning sheet such as that shown in Figure 2 can be helpful; this particular example involves the participant's supervisor in the planning sequence.

Follow-Up Activities

Follow-up activities fall into two categories: (1) those involving reminders, either sent from the trainer to individual participants or sent or delivered to each participant by a buddy, and (2) those involving subsequent meetings of the original group of participants.

Nadler (1976c) describes a follow-up mechanism that consists of memos from the participants to themselves; these memos, which are written during training sessions and are designed to remind the participants of the actions they planned to take as a result of training, are given to the trainer for mailing to participants at a later date. Another follow-up approach is to ask the participants to plan how they will report on the workshop to their co-workers and supervisors (Nadler, 1976c). When participants undertake such a planning effort during a workshop, not only are they better prepared for the questions and discussions that may arise when they return to work, but they also develop a clearer picture of the most important aspects of the program.

Another useful follow-up mechanism is the mailing of relevant materials to participants. These materials may include readings, bibliographies, fliers on related programs, and notes of encouragement to keep journals and to document on-the-job learnings.

TRAINING & DEVELOPMENT
ACTION PLAN

Program Title	Program Date

As a result of this training, I want to START doing: STOP doing: KEEP doing:	How I will measure my success:

My supervisor and I have agreed to the following to help me meet my goals:

Signature of Participant	Signature of Supervisor	Date

Keep one copy and give one copy to your supervisor for future assessment of progress (follow-up discussion and/or performance review).

Figure 2. Example of an Action-Planning Sheet[2]

---

[2]Reprinted with the permission of Analog Devices in Norwood, Massachusetts.

Example: Using mailings sent to participants as a program follow-up.

At the request of the director, a trainer presented a one-session program on performance evaluation and feedback to all of the managers and supervisors in a department. Two months later, just prior to the company-wide annual performance-evaluation discussions, the trainer sent packets of materials to all program participants.

The packets contained a list of the characteristics of effective performance-evaluation discussions (which had been generated by the participants), an article on common problems that supervisors encounter when conducting performance-review discussions, and a form to be used to help organize thoughts in preparation for the discussion sessions. A cover letter suggested that the participants refer to their original action-planning sheets from the workshop; it also encouraged them to implement the changes that they had identified as desirable and to talk with their own supervisors about their efforts.

Trost (1985) writes that to encourage the transfer of learning, follow-up sessions should be designed as opportunities to tackle problems that have emerged from participants' efforts to apply learnings, rather than as forums to introduce new content areas. He cautions that in follow-up activities, just as in the initial training, a chance to practice and receive feedback is essential.

6

Evaluating Training

Most trainers attempt some kind of program evaluation. For example, participant reaction sheets are *de rigueur* for many programs. However, some trainers are intimidated by formal evaluations of program effectiveness and feel inadequately versed in the technologies available. It may be helpful to remember that program evaluation does not have to be one's personal nemesis and can, instead, be an ally. The key to careful, thorough, nonthreatening evaluation lies in planning the evaluation effort during the needs-assessment and program-design stages. Evaluation processes should be integrated into program design as carefully as program content.

RATIONALE AND OBJECTIVES

Depending on a trainer's exposure to and expertise with different methods of evaluation, the process can be more or less complex. Effective evaluation can be useful in several ways:

1. It can provide a gauge of how well the objective of changing the participants' knowledge, attitude, or skill level is being accomplished (Newstrom, 1975).
2. It can generate feedback for trainers and designers that can be used for improving, upgrading, or redesigning a program (Komras, 1985; Nadler, 1976c; Swierczek & Carmichael, 1985).
3. It can offer the trainer a way of monitoring his or her own performance.
4. It can increase the credibility of the training function (Zenger & Hargis, 1982). People tend to respect an organization that openly evaluates its efforts and tries to improve its effectiveness.

5. It can provide management with information about the value and the costs of training. Evaluation data can be used to support not only successful programs but also efforts to improve less-successful programs. As Zenger and Hargis (1982, p. 11) note, "Experience shows that in times of crisis or downturn, training budgets are often among the first to be cut. . . . Until good research is provided, management support will be based primarily on faith and emotions, which can change radically!" Therefore, evaluation is critical to the survival of many training functions.

EVALUATION METHODS

Training literature offers many theories, schema, theoretical frameworks, and practical techniques for evaluating training methods. For example, Kirkpatrick (1979) presents a useful framework involving four areas of evaluation: (1) reactions of participants; (2) learning of knowledge, skills, and attitudes; (3) behavior on the job; and (4) results. Merwin (1981), in contrast, states that there are basically four elements in classroom training experiences, all of which should be evaluated: (1) the trainer, (2) the content, (3) the participants, and (4) the environment and facilities.

Methods of evaluation range from simple, on-the-spot questions asked by the trainer to elaborate, computer-analyzed, multifaceted data matrices. However, complexity of method is not necessarily related to effectiveness. Depending on their purpose and appropriateness, simple methods can provide as much usable information as more complex ones. Some trainers are intimidated by their belief that they lack the necessary sophistication to conduct evaluations and, therefore, do not use the methods that will provide the information they need. Others are impressed with and choose esoteric formats and gain very little useful information. The crucial factor in selecting the appropriate method of evaluation is clarity about who is to do the evaluation, for whom the evaluation data are being generated, how the data will be used, and what kinds of data will be useful. Consequently, the first step is to think through the process.

The most common evaluation methods discussed in the literature include participant reports; measures of changes in knowledge, skill, attitudes, or performance; trainer reports; and observer reports.

Participant Reports

An anonymous, end-of-session, participant-reaction sheet is the evaluation device used most frequently. Such forms are often called "smile sheets" or "happiness quotients" (Nadler, 1976c) because participants usually are asked to report on the extent to which they liked the training. However, reaction sheets can explore other issues, including to what extent the participants feel that their expectations were met as well as their impressions of the thoroughness of the content and the effectiveness of the presenter.

Although this kind of sheet is popular, it presents several difficulties. Because many participants have no previous training experiences to use as a basis of comparison, evaluations sometimes take place in a vacuum; as a result a program may be evaluated uniformly high, and useful critical comments may not be offered. Sometimes participants react to the last activity or concept presented and base their reaction-sheet answers on how they feel at the end of the program instead of on the entire experience. Many participants could be more objective if they had a chance to distance themselves from a program before completing an evaluation form. However, when participants are allowed to leave with their reaction sheets, they often fail to return them; consequently, the trainer loses valuable feedback. Another problem is that questions on reaction sheets are frequently worded ambiguously and do not elicit useful data. In addition, at the end of a program the participants sometimes are so eager to leave that they complete their reaction sheets superficially.

However, with careful wording and a mixture of types of items (for example, multiple choice, fill in, and true or false), reaction sheets can provide useful data. The example provided in Figure 3 is intended to be used at the end of a seminar (Merwin, 1981). It is longer than most reaction sheets and uses several types of questions and asks for further clarification when the respondent answers "no."

EVALUATION FORM

	Evaluation	
	Yes	*No*
1. Was it your choice to attend this workshop?	_____	_____
2. Did you listen attentively to the information presented?	_____	_____

If you responded NO to question 2, explain:

_____

3. Did you arrive on time and return from breaks punctually?   _____ _____

If you responded NO, explain:_____

_____

4. Did you participate willingly in the work- shop activities?   _____ _____

If you responded NO, explain:_____

_____

5. Did you have an acceptable attitude that facilitated learning?   _____ _____

If NO, explain: _____

_____

6. Did the seminar leader allow time for questions?   _____ _____

If you answered NO, did you ask the leader questions?

Yes _____   No _____

Figure 3. Example of an End-of-Seminar Evaluation Form[3]

---

[3]From *Effective Evaluation Strategies and Techniques: A Key to Successful Training* (p. 24) by Sandra Merwin, 1986, San Diego, CA: University Associates. Copyright 1986 by University Associates. Reprinted by permission.

	Evaluation	
	Yes	No

7. Did the seminar leader explain and clarify his or her information?   _____   _____

   If NO, did you ask the leader to clarify or explain further?

   Yes _____ No _____

8. Did the seminar leader speak clearly and distinctly?   _____   _____

   If NO, explain: _____

   _____

9. Did the seminar leader keep the training session moving and on course?   _____   _____

   If NO, explain: _____

   _____

10. Did the instructor demonstrate a thorough knowledge of the topic?   _____   _____

    If NO, explain: _____

    _____

11. Was the following objective covered in this seminar? (Objective 1)   _____   _____

    If NO, explain: _____

    _____

12. Was the following objective covered in this seminar? (Objective 2)   _____   _____

    If NO, explain: _____

    _____

Figure 3 (continued). Example of an End-of-Seminar Evaluation Form

	Evaluation	
	Yes	*No*
13. Was the following objective covered in this seminar? (Objective 3)	_____	_____
If NO, explain: _____		
_____		
14. Was the following objective covered in this seminar? (Objective 4)	_____	_____
If NO, explain: _____		
_____		
15. Was the course content clearly organized and well prepared?	_____	_____
If NO, explain: _____		
_____		
16. Were the facilities adequate?	_____	_____
If NO, explain: _____		
_____		

17. Rate this workshop. Please circle one:

Poor   Fair   Good   Very Good   Excellent

18. Please add general comments:_____

_____

_____

Figure 3 (continued). Example of an End-of-Seminar Evaluation Form

Reaction sheets may be used during a program or at the end of certain sessions as a check on content relevance and presenter effectiveness. Participant reactions provide information that allows trainers to redesign subsequent sessions to meet needs more adequately.

Participant reactions can also be collected through interviews. To gather data, the trainer or the program evaluator may conduct interviews with a sample of program participants. Those being interviewed may be asked to relate anecdotal evidence to demonstrate their use of workshop learnings on the job.

Measures of Changes

Measures of change are traditionally associated with evaluation efforts. However, change indices involve study over time; and training evaluations are not typically longitudinal. Swierczek and Carmichael (1985) cite the lack of access to participants and the nonexistence of baseline information as the usual reasons for not doing long-term studies. They point out that without baseline data, it is difficult to be certain that changes are linked to the training provided.

Pretesting and posttesting can measure whether or not learning has occurred; but, as Swierczek and Carmichael (1985) write, the changes measured do not indicate whether transfer of learning is occurring. Merwin (1981) suggests using different pretests and posttests of program content; if two questions are developed for every topic, one can appear on the pretest and one on the posttest.

Del Gaizo (1984) suggests including job- or task-simulation activities in workshops so that performance can be observed and evaluated by fellow participants. These activities can be conducted both before and after training. Kelley, Orgel, and Baer (1984) suggest examining data that have already been collected within the organization (for example, sales records, absent/tardy records, work quality, and quantity of work) and comparing these statistics before and after training.

Trainer Reports

After completing a program, many trainers make notes to themselves about effectiveness, changes for subsequent presentations, and questions or issues raised. Merwin (1981) suggests that trainers record their own perceptions by using a format similar to that used for participant evaluations. Use of a standard form at the end of each program ensures consistency and thoroughness of trainer evaluation across programs. Also, if several trainers make presentations during the program, they may be interviewed or surveyed; the resulting data may be useful in improving program effectiveness.

Observer Reports

Training evaluators or observers can aid the evaluation process. Tyson and Birnbauer (1985) suggest that evaluators use check lists to record their observations and to clarify their responses.

In some training units, certain individuals have responsibility for program evaluation. In very small training units, peer review of a specific program can sometimes be arranged in a reciprocal agreement with other training units.

CONSTRUCTING EVALUATION INSTRUMENTS

Evaluation processes often include instruments. The usefulness of the data produced is determined by the questions or items that are used and the way in which they are phrased. Unless items are constructed to generate the kinds of data wanted, evaluation becomes a wasted opportunity.

Before constructing an evaluation instrument, the trainer must think clearly about the kind of information that is desired and how it will be used. To determine whether the wording is clear and unambiguous, it is a good idea to develop a draft and show it to colleagues, friends, and relatives. Sometimes an instrument can be pretested. In addition, the trainer may discuss the instrument with participants after they have completed it to see if they had any difficulties with particular items or with the overall tone.

Del Gaizo (1984) cautions that questions need to be carefully worded, that topics should be measured one at a time, and that forced-choice responses must be mutually exclusive and exhaustive. The entire questionnaire should take less than twenty minutes to complete.

PROBLEMS ENCOUNTERED
WITH EVALUATION METHODS

Tracey (1984) lists several common causes of problems in conducting evaluations. He cites inadequate planning (including failure to work out details, to train evaluators, and to make the purposes and recommendations clear); improper interpretation of findings; inappropriate use of the results; evaluation errors (including instrument items that are written in ways that cause different perceptions of meaning and therefore are ranked by different methods); and lack of objectivity on the part of the evaluator or in the instrument itself.

Nadler (1976c, pp. 33-34) points out that timing in the use of an instrument has an effect on the results produced: "Obviously there is no best way or time to evaluate. The variety of possibilities should be weighed against the objectives as to why the evaluation is taking place, the nature of the participants, and what will be done with the data."

ANALYSIS OF DATA

As mentioned earlier in this chapter, before data are collected the trainer must carefully consider how they will be analyzed and to whom they will be distributed. Surveys and interviews can be constructed and conducted in ways that allow easy compilation and analysis of the data. If the evaluation form will be analyzed on a computer, help from computer experts in designing the form may save time during the data-entry phase.

Frequency counts of participants' responses in specified ways can be useful (for example, the number of participants who indicated that a program was too short and needed more sessions). In addition, the percent of responses to various choices can reveal useful comparative data (for example, the percent of participants who thought a program accurately reflected the descriptive materials and objectives distributed prior to the first session). Statistical analysis and graphic analysis (Kelley, Orgel, & Baer, 1984) are other ways to analyze the data produced.

A formal report on the outcome of training may benefit from supportive statistics if the presenter is well versed in their meanings and the limitations of how they can be interpreted; but again, the kind of analysis chosen should depend on how the data will be used. Nadler (1976c) suggests that data can be shared with participants via a newsletter in an effort to reinforce the workshop experience after the participants have returned to their jobs. The data might be shared in a report that summarizes the participants' comments and the changes they would like to see in the program. Feedback to an individual presenter could include comments from the participants on his or her presentation but exclude comments about other presenters. Senior management might be most interested in a table comparing the effectiveness of different programs across divisions.

Trapnell (1984, p. 90) points out that a training effort should be assessed as a whole and asks, "In what environmental and political context does it exist?" Because the effectiveness of training is influenced by the tone, leadership, and economic conditions of the company, evaluation results need to be considered within these contexts.

7

Selecting Presenters

Those who present or lead training sessions provide opportunities for fruitful learning experiences and become catalysts for growth. Whether these people come from within or outside an organization, they and their skills in communicating are as important as the focus and content of a training program. Vibrant, relevant, and cutting-edge information can be rendered dead by an unenthusiastic, rigid presentation. On the other hand, a skillful individual can supply little content and yet lead participants in discovering their own expertise and increasing their self-esteem and confidence in the process.

USING INTERNAL RESOURCES

In the name of cost consciousness, many organizations retain very few internal training professionals. It makes financial sense to find ways to tap existing expertise for presentations in training programs. A solo or part-time trainer can accomplish more if others throughout the organization share in the responsibility of training. In addition to expertise in his or her particular area of interest, an internal presenter often has an enormous amount of information about the organization and how it works. This knowledge can add relevance to a presentation. Also, the presenter's reputation within the organization and his or her understanding of how a program's content specifically applies to that organization can increase the credibility of the program. Participants cannot deny the existence of a phenomenon by saying, "That doesn't happen here" when the presenter can say from personal knowledge or experience that it does.

Example: Using internal presenters to increase program credibility.

The upper management of a Fortune 500 company was disturbed by an increase in complaints about racist comments and jokes on the job. A memo that reiterated the existing policies against harassment was distributed to all mid-level managers.

Upper management continued to receive complaints and decided to implement a training program. In the first session, many of the participants expressed disbelief that harassment was occurring. In the second session, the personnel director presented a list of anonymous racist remarks that had been overheard by several individuals. The personnel director also related some of the measures used to deal with those who had originated the remarks. The participants began to accept the reality of the existence of racism in their organization because of their exposure to information from a reliable and credible source.

The use of credible resources as presenters can reduce resistance to training within the organization. As Christensen and Kinlaw (1984) write:

Participant resistance to the training can be reduced if managers are involved in the design, delivery and evaluation of the program. When trainees know their colleagues and supervisors have a major role in the program and responsibility for its success, they are open to the value of the program because they accept its credibility. Not only do trainees perceive the manager-trainers as credible, they receive confirmation that the company supports the content of the program. (p. 89)

When an organization uses internal presenters, both the participants and the presenters themselves can benefit from the increased visibility and exposure that they experience. The participants have an opportunity to see and be seen by members of management and others with whom they have no contact in the normal course of their jobs and whom they may not have even met. In addition, members of senior management are often seen as more accessible after they make presentations in training programs. Another advantage is that various facets of organizational culture can be demonstrated rather than just discussed.

Example: Using a panel of managers as a living example of organizational culture.

A design team that was working on the development of a training program for mid-level managers wanted to communicate the company's commitment to increasing diversity among the work force. During one of the sessions, the team invited a panel of senior managers to talk about organizational culture. The composition of the panel reflected the organizational value of diversity because it included males, females, minorities, and people of different ages. Seeing the diversity in senior management was more convincing than just hearing about it would have been.

Managers who serve as presenters often find that this experience increases their awareness of organizational issues. Sometimes the sharing of information that takes place during training leads to action steps that correct problems. Christensen and Kinlaw (1984) talk about this phenomenon as increasing the impact of training:

> The first benefit that an organization can receive from involving its managers in every phase of management training programs is that training programs can be transformed into organizational development interventions. Not only do the participants learn new knowledge and skills, but organizational values, practices and policies can be influenced. The new insight and commitment of managers who assume responsibility for a program lever the training into an instrument of organizational change.
>
> For example, we recently involved managers in designing and conducting a performance appraisal workshop. The managers responsible for the program became so aware of their system's weaknesses and the pervasiveness of poor appraisal practices that the company launched a massive appraisal training effort for all employees, developed a new set of guidelines for using the system and issued a new policy on performance management. (p. 87)

Finding Internal Presenters

Some training programs are primarily oriented toward communicating specific information to participants. In such cases the trainer can capitalize on the widespread content expertise that already exists within an organization. Processes can be developed to identify organizational members who might be potential program presenters.

Some experts, of course, are not able to communicate their knowledge to others. A computer whiz once said that he could present any information, no matter how technical, to a console—but not to a human. Content expertise does not predict ability to teach or even ability to communicate enthusiasm for the subject. There are usually several people in an organization with the knowledge to make a presentation on a specific content area, but the trainer must carefully consider who is best able to talk with groups when choosing among possible presenters.

Example: Considering communication skills when choosing a presenter.

A training manager was designing an informational program about a soon-to-be-installed telephone system. The director of telecommunications was a brilliant woman who was nationally known for her development of cutting-edge communications systems but who was unable to explain concepts simply and concisely. Her assistant was much better at relating to people. The training manager weighed the added status of the director's participation in the program against the increased clarity of communication and enthusiasm that would be provided by the assistant. He asked the assistant to make the presentation but tried to compensate by arranging for a cameo appearance by the director.

The needs-assessment process can be used to identify individuals who might be able to make presentations. During interviews people may be asked to identify those who might be good presenters and those who are the best managers, and individuals who are repeatedly suggested can be considered as potential presenters. It is important not to raise expectations that someone who is suggested will be asked to make a presentation; the fact that a person wants to be a presenter is no guarantee that he or she will be effective.

The trainer often needs to obtain the approval of an employee's manager before asking that employee to make a presentation. Many managers are quite willing for their employees to be presenters; they realize that the presentations will generate increased visibility for their departments. However, any manager might be disconcerted to discover after the fact that an employee has made a presentation.

In addition to sharing specific expertise in programs, internal resources can be used in other ways. For example, to add status to a program, members of senior management can be asked to serve as members of a panel. However, because there are limits to how frequently their participation should be requested, the trainer must thoughtfully choose them for programs in which their impact will be most useful. The auxiliary messages that their presentations may send to program participants should be considered, and the focus and timing of the session should be chosen to maximize the achievement of the program goals.

Enlisting the aid of line managers in developing and presenting programs can also be beneficial. This is one way to publicly recognize individuals who are viewed as the best managers. In addition, having several managers form a panel to publicly discuss a relevant issue implies that the organization values their perceptions and input. Preparing and presenting can also be a development opportunity for the managers. As Christensen and Kinlaw (1984) say:

> Another benefit to the organization that results from the extensive involvement of managers in management training is a multiplication of training outcomes. Managers who serve as trainers will learn more about their topic through the experience of training others and become committed to applying what they teach in their own work groups. Simply stated, the organization not only develops the managers who are *being* trained, it also develops the managers who *do* the training. (p. 87)

The added visibility gained by a manager who makes a presentation can change perceptions of his or her function in the organization.

Example: Using visibility as a presenter to expand a manager's organizational role.

The director of an employee-assistance program regularly makes a presentation in a program that was developed for new supervisors. Although the director is usually seen in the company as a resource for troubled employees, in the program he stresses his willingness to work with the supervisors of these employees and to help them deal earlier and more effectively with difficult situations. He lets the supervisors know that they can use his services as a consultant in forming strategies to deal with such situations. Consequently, he has used his duties as a presenter to expand his role in the organization.

Training and Supporting Internal Presenters

In order to capitalize on internal expertise, the trainer needs to devote time and attention to developing presenters. The amount of time necessary will depend on the extent of the presenters' roles in programs, their ability to communicate comfortably in front of groups, their self-confidence, and the extent of their knowledge of styles of adult learning and presentation techniques. If someone is giving a brief, informational talk on a specific topic and is quite skillful in engaging and holding participants' interest, little attention needs to be paid to developing that person's presentation skills. However, if a small group of managers is asked to design and present a talk on development opportunities for mid-level managers, a lot of thought and time may be needed to increase the managers' skills.

Working with people to improve their skills and comfort in making presentations is a very tricky business. Even those individuals who sincerely want feedback and guidance are sometimes defensive about their styles. Another difficulty is that presenters often do not have formal responsibility for training and feel that they are doing the company or trainer a favor. However, since both the presenter's and the training department's reputations are on the line when a presentation is made, it is important to find tactful and mutually acceptable ways to maximize the effectiveness of that presentation.

One way to increase the likelihood that people will listen to feedback about their presentation styles is to comment on the content of their presentations as well as on their delivery. Praise on the extent of someone's knowledge of a subject can be combined with suggestions for alternative ways to present the information. Presenters can be assisted in planning strategies for presenting the information in ways that will maximize the audience's understanding.

Trainers can co-train with individuals in order to combine content expertise with skills in designing, organizing, and training. Also, presenters can be educated on how to make decisions about structuring presentations and on what issues and group processes to consider; co-designing with advisory groups can increase presenters' awareness of these issues. Taking an active role in developing people as presenters serves another useful purpose: it increases their awareness of the trainer's skills and of the time and effort necessary to produce effective programs.

Because people are sometimes more receptive to feedback from an external expert than from a peer, the trainer may want to have an external consultant lead a workshop on effective presentations. The trainer may decide to participate in the workshop if it appears that his or her role modeling of receiving and using feedback would be beneficial to the group. If senior management acknowledges these efforts to refine their presentations, the participants may view this as a desirable opportunity. Trainers can attend presentations and afterward talk to the presenters about what went right and what could have been done differently. Comments and ratings from participant evaluation sheets may be shared, and ways to integrate useful ideas and criticisms may be discussed.

Perhaps the most useful tool to increase presenters' self-awareness is videotape. Regardless of how much verbal feedback people receive on their presentations, it is more enlightening for them to see themselves in action. Video is a powerful intervention that needs to be used within a context of trust and with ample preparation and follow-up. Although individuals can learn a lot from watching themselves on tape, they usually need help in integrating and interpreting what they see. Therefore, this technique must be used carefully with much thought and planning.

On one end of a continuum are people who present brief, informational pieces once in a program; on the other end are managers who learn to be trainers and change agents in their organizations. The trainer can help both types of individuals—as well as those in between—to become more aware of organizational issues, to increase their skills of observation and influence, and to thereby increase their effectiveness in promoting change within the organization.

Acknowledging the Efforts of Internal Presenters

Expressing sincere appreciation for the presenters' efforts is extremely valuable to a training and development function. Different organizations have different policies, procedures, and norms regarding what is allowed and what is preferred in terms of acknowledgment and appreciation. Although trainers need to be aware of such rules and norms, they also should try to be creative and sincere in their expressions of gratitude. Some organizations require reimbursement to the home department for the time that an employee devotes to presentations; some allow payment to personnel for efforts that are outside their normal job functions; and some ban additional payment of any kind to full-time employees. Whatever form of acknowledgment is chosen must be seen as positive within the organization.

Regardless of other forms of appreciation, the trainer can send a letter of acknowledgment to each presenter and a copy to his or her immediate supervisor. Many trainers send a small token of appreciation at the end of the year to everyone who has made presentations during that year (for example, a pair of movie passes, a book, a company T-shirt, or a gift certificate). Others hold a reception for all presenters at the end of the year and invite senior managers to thank them.

The political implications of letters of appreciation to senior management (listing those individuals who made presentations) should be considered. This kind of acknowledgment increases the visibility of the shared responsibility for training within an organization, but senior management and individual presenters may or may not see this as an advantage. The trainer must be sure that such letters will not only communicate appreciation but also be welcomed.

USING EXTERNAL CONSULTANTS

One strategy for supplementing a small, internal training staff is to hire external consultants for specific training assignments. This practice can significantly expand the scope and number of programs offered.

Although at times external consultants' credibility is questioned because "They don't *really* understand our unique situation," at other times they are granted credibility that an internal member of a training staff is not. If a recognized expert is brought in to consult, frequently members of the organization will see value in information that they dismissed when presented by an internal source. Therefore, there may be times when using an outside person is a particularly good strategy. For instance, when the message in a program is radically different or controversial in an organization, it might be better for the ideas to come from a source that will not continue to try to exist within that organization.

Finding External Consultants

There are many ways to obtain names of consultants, and it is probably best to use several sources. Although the trainer should be creative in the search, the following suggestions may be helpful:

- Talk to other trainers and training organizations within similar companies. Find out who used whom for what and whether those being questioned would rehire the same consultants if other opportunities arose.
- Talk to the leaders of local and national training organizations to generate more names. Be candid and specific and elicit advice. Also inquire about any concerns or reservations people might have about recommending certain individuals.
- Look for trainers' names in community college catalogs, listings of certificate programs, course listings for continuing education or for YMCAs or YWCAs, announcements of private workshops, and similar brochures.
- Look through local and national membership rolls of professional organizations.
- Notice who is active in presenting development opportunities for professional organizations.
- See who has written or is mentioned in articles in trade magazines and newsletters.
- Call well-known experts whose fees you cannot afford, and obtain their recommendations of reasonably priced consultants.

Example: Using creative methods to find consultants.

A manager asked Ben, the training director, to suggest someone to help his department to become more productive in staff meetings and in work teams. Ben could not find an appropriate consultant through his usual channels. He knew that Catherine, a professor at a local university, was a well-known expert on process consultation, team building, and helping people to function better in work groups. Although Ben had never met Catherine and knew he could not afford to hire her, he telephoned her. When he explained the situation, she suggested that he hire a team of her graduate students; and she said that she would personally supervise these students. After several meetings and much discussion, a contract was developed and the students did the work. The arrangement worked well, and the professor became a valuable resource and colleague for the training director.

Interviewing External Consultants

After identifying several consultants, the next step is making appointments to talk with them. It is a good idea to let the consultant talk as much as possible. A consultant should feel comfortable enough in an interview situation to put others at ease; an inability to engage in a lively and relaxed interview should make the trainer question that consultant's effectiveness in front of a group. The following guidelines might be helpful in interviewing consultants:

- Interview the consultant who will actually make the presentation. A first meeting is often with a marketing representative who will not be at the training event. When dealing with a large consulting firm, find out who will actually do the training.
- Notice what the consultant asks.
- Think about the kinds of information that the consultant needs in order to conduct the specific training program involved. Become suspicious if the consultant does not ask the appropriate questions to generate the information needed.
- Discuss the types of information that will be needed as a standard (for example, goals for the event, specifics about the audience, the origin of the request for training, the number of participants, where the training will occur, and what the facilities will consist of). Notice what the consultant is curious about and what he or she must be assuming. This kind of analysis will provide clues about how tailored the presentation is likely to be. For instance, if a consultant who will be conducting a workshop on improving customer relations does not ask what specific kinds of customers cause the most frequent problems, then the cases used for discussion in the workshop will be generic rather than tailored.

Obtaining References

Trainers may find the following suggestions helpful in obtaining references for external consultants:

- Obtain references from several sources.
- Contact other training professionals who know a consultant's work and determine the context of their associations with the consultant (for example, teacher, co-trainer, or employer).
- Ask people who hired a consultant if they would use him or her again.
- Request some references from organizations in which a consultant has worked repeatedly or for a long time. It is reasonable to be nervous about someone who has worked only once for many organizations.
- Contact people who have been participants in workshops or other events conducted by the consultant.
- Try to obtain references from organizations as similar as possible to your own. Even a consultant who is a good platform presenter will not be effective if he or she is unable to relate to members of a particular industry.

Example: The importance of understanding the audience.

A director of training tried for a long time to find a consultant to teach presentation skills to research and computer personnel in a large, high-tech firm. A particular consultant's name appeared repeatedly by recommendation, in published articles in professional journals and in brochures introducing him as a presenter at professional meetings. The director hired the consultant to do a pilot program for a select, influential group of employees.

The consultant had usually worked with groups of mental-health workers and teachers. Many participants in the high-tech firm were put off by the kinds of examples he used, the way he structured the sessions, and his lack of understanding of technical jargon. This knowledgeable consultant's lack of understanding of his audience and his inability to apply his own teachings about "knowing your audience" negatively influenced the participants' ability to learn.

Seeing an External Consultant in Action

Usually it is not possible to determine from an interview alone how well a consultant will perform. Whenever possible, the person who hires the consultant should watch him or her in action.

Example: Differences between what consultants say they do and what they actually do.

Two training professionals, Bert and Jackie, secured the services of a consultant with a specific area of expertise. This consultant had been recommended highly by people they knew, including a senior training professional whom they both respected. The consultant's marketing pitch was polished and clear-cut. When the well-publicized and highly visible pilot program was presented, the consultant failed miserably. He delivered no more content than he had communicated as an outline of his presentation. In addition, he used blatantly sexist examples in his presentation. After the fiasco, Bert and Jackie kept a low profile for a while to give their disappointment, their anger, and the tarnish on their reputations time to fade.

If a consultant is very resistant to observation, a prospective client has a right to be suspicious. If the consultant cannot allow someone to observe because of client restrictions, then a complimentary or short, inexpensive training session might be arranged. If the consultant agrees to such a session, people who will be able to help gauge his or her potential for success should be invited to attend. Careful decisions should be made about whom to invite and whom not to invite; repercussions from excluding particular individuals from the decision-making process can be as serious as those from including the wrong people.

Hiring an External Consultant

There are a number of issues to consider when hiring an outside consultant. This section is addressed to the person who will be doing the hiring.

The first step is to learn about the established policies and procedures within the organization. In all likelihood, someone has hired a consultant before. People within the company to talk to may include supervisors, the purchasing officer, or someone in the personnel department. Also, it is important to find out who is responsible for overseeing the contractual and financial commitments involved in hiring a consultant. Typically, the following questions need to be answered:

- Who has the authority to send letters of commitment or to sign contracts? Who needs to countersign?
- What backup is necessary to ensure payment to the consultant (for example, biographical information, vitae, written recommendations, or proposals)?
- What other specific information or signatures are needed?
- Is it necessary to investigate to determine whether the fee is a usual and customary amount? (It is a good idea to check what others in the field are paid as consultants. Professional organizations can provide a usual range of fees.)
- Can (or should) the consultant be paid before the work has been completed or only on the basis of invoices submitted after completion?
- What are the consultant's billing procedures?
- Does the consultant bill exclusively for training time or for planning, design, and travel time as well?
- Are there different fees for the different uses of time? Is planning time less expensive than actual presentation time?
- Does it cost less to go to the consultant's office for planning sessions than to have him or her come to your office?
- How has the consultant structured a fee schedule? Does he or she bill for the number of hours of a presentation or for days and fractions of days?
- What expenses will be charged? Will the consultant charge for travel expenses and travel time? Will an estimate of expenses be submitted?
- Who provides and pays for materials and services such as photocopies, films, audiovisual equipment, handouts, instruments, and the scoring of instruments?
- What other equipment will be needed (for example, newsprint, flip charts, felt-tipped markers, and masking tape)?
- Do the fee schedules differ for profit and not-for-profit organizations?
- Are the rates negotiable?

When using one consultant a great deal, it might make financial sense to inquire about paying on the basis of a time-bound retainer rather than a fee-for-service schedule. For example, the consultant might be asked how much would be charged on the basis of a commitment to use him or her for a certain number of hours per month for an entire year. Sometimes a consultant will charge less per hour to obtain a commitment in advance for a specified amount of work. One of the hardest things about being a consultant is becoming accustomed to the irregular nature of the work flow; therefore, some consultants like arrangements that give them a long-term commitment of a known number of hours or days. A long-term commitment saves time on renegotiating contracts, so it actually costs the consultant less. Nevertheless, before investigating this scheme with a consultant, it is important to ensure that company policies allow this kind of arrangement and that the demand for the consultant's service will continue for the duration of the contract.

One of the most common problems in the use of outside consultants involves supervision. Consultants can be only as good as they are helped to be. Trainers need to be very clear about goals and expectations for a project; consultants must be told, as explicitly as possible, what is expected of them and what outcomes are desired. Someone must be assigned the responsibility for defining the project and supervising and evaluating a consultant's work; in addition, someone should be responsible for observing the sessions and critiquing them with the consultant. It is essential to provide very basic and very clear guidelines of what behaviors are expected; for example, a consultant should be told whether he or she is expected to supply all handouts or to submit invoices on completion of work. The more that is spelled out, the more likely it is that the relationship will be a satisfying one. It is better to err on the side of being too explicit rather than to leave things to chance and thereby increase the possibility of a misunderstanding. The consultant should be given any nonproprietary information that will help him or her to understand the context of the organization and increase his or her ability to relate to group members.

DEVELOPING SYSTEMS AND FORMS

Systems can be developed to track information involved in running programs. Where contracts and money are concerned, it is especially important to be clear about agreements and to have easy access to information. Files on potential presenters can be developed with information about their areas of expertise, their accomplishments, their reputations, and their fee schedules if they are external consultants.

In gathering information on presenter preferences, the trainer should record answers to the following types of questions:

- What is the minimum number of participants that the presenter requires for sessions? What is the maximum number that he or she allows?
- What are the presenter's requirements regarding the physical setting? Are tables or movable chairs necessary?
- What equipment will the presenter need?

Although some of these questions may not be applicable for internal presenters, they should always be considered. Forms can be designed to track all of the information that is gathered (see Figure 4). Program-proposal forms are also very valuable tools (see Figure 5). Copies of necessary organizational forms (consultant agreement forms, patent-copyright agreements, and so forth) should be readily accessible.

PILOT PROGRAMS

A pilot program is a lot like an out-of-town opening of a Broadway play. It provides an opportunity to try a program, iron out kinks, receive feedback, and be forgiven for mistakes. It can also build the confidence of those backing it, promoting it, starring in it, and buying tickets to see it. If a program survives and flourishes at the pilot stage, it is probably a winner.

A pilot can offer a chance to try a new consultant or presenter or to see someone in action in the organization. Gauging the reactions of the audience and helping the presenter to fine-tune the program to meet the goals can pay dividends.

A pilot also can offer an opportunity to try something new in an arena that is less visible and risky than that of the final program. In the absense of heralding trumpets, new and different approaches can be tried with less scrutiny. It is also possible in a pilot to make mistakes that would not be forgotten or forgiven in the final program. In addition, a pilot can be used to increase the commitment to a program on the part of particular segments of the population.

PRESENTER-INFORMATION FORM

Name _____

Company _____

Company Address_____

_____

Company Phone Number _____

Home Address _____

_____

Home Phone Number_____

Social Security No. _____

Business Federal Tax No._____

Preferences:
  Number of Participants _____

  Physical Setting _____

  Other _____

  _____

  _____

  _____

Costs:
  Date _____ Rate _____ Other Costs _____

  Date _____ Rate _____ Other Costs _____

  Date _____ Rate _____ Other Costs _____

Figure 4. Example of a Presenter-Information Form

PROGRAM-PROPOSAL FORM

Tentative Title of Program _____

Major Presenters

   1. Name_____

      Organization_____

      Address _____

      _____

      _____

      Phone Number_____

   2. Name_____

      Organization_____

      Address _____

      _____

      _____

      Phone Number_____

   3. Name_____

      Organization_____

      Address _____

      _____

      _____

      Phone Number_____

Figure 5. Example of a Program-Proposal Form

Other Possible Presenters _____

Explanation and/or Description _____

_____

_____

_____

_____

Participants (number and restrictions) _____

_____

_____

_____

_____

When (number of sessions, dates, length of sessions, preferred time of day) _____

_____

_____

_____

_____

Where (preferences for room, chairs, tables, chalkboard, audiovisuals, reading materials, etc.) _____

_____

_____

_____

Figure 5 (continued). Example of a Program-Proposal Form

Costs _____

Protocol/Permission _____

Other _____

_____

_____

_____

_____

Figure 5 (continued). Example of a Program-Proposal Form

Example: Using a pilot program to increase the commitment of resistant segments of the population.

A training manager wanted to provide training programs for long-term supervisors. Experience had shown that a large portion of the organization's grievances were a direct result of lack of skill on the part of supervisors. However, the training manager could not require people to attend training sessions. Consequently, to entice long-term supervisors to experience the value of attending supervisory-training programs, she purposely invited an outspoken group to attend and evaluate a pilot of one new program. Under the guise of being critics, many of the supervisors found the experience personally helpful and enjoyed the opportunity to address some thorny supervisory issues.

On occasion, a manager expects a specific training program to help an individual with a performance problem. Some people are more receptive to learning if they are asked to help evaluate the worth of a program than they are if they are told to attend because they need the training. An indirect approach can be useful in situations in which people need to save face. For example, a mid-level manager lacking basic writing skills can be invited to attend a writing-skills workshop to determine whether it is suitable for his or her staff.

There are also disadvantages to a pilot. It can cost as much in dollars, time, and effort as a final program. Also, it does not have the added benefit of increased exposure and credibility for the training function. In addition, participants in a pilot sometimes do not take the content as seriously as they do when they are involved in a final program.

The issue of who should be invited to a pilot needs a great deal of thought. If critical feedback is desired, then those invited should not be solely the "program junkies" (who see only the benefits of training) and the people who are already committed to the particular program. At the same time, the trainer must realize that being part of a less-than-perfect program can permanently alienate some people. The sample group should be chosen to reflect the audience to which the program will ultimately be marketed.

A TRAINER'S ROLE AS A RESOURCE BANK

As a collector of information about finding and using internal and external presenters, about consultants with specific expertise, and about networks that can provide names of consultants, a trainer can be a wonderful resource for members of an organization. For instance, if a unit wants to create a training event or is responsible for a professional meeting, a trainer's knowledge can be very useful. Even if a specific presenter cannot be located for the unit, help can be obtained in understanding the procedures, policies, and recommended methods to find, use, supervise, and evaluate presenters. These skills can be useful frequently—or at odd times—in organizational life.

Example: Using a training manager as a resource for consultants.

A vice president of a medium-sized company chaired a powerful committee in a professional scientific association. His company had benefited from this exposure and had closed several important business deals with other association members. When the national meeting was scheduled to be held in his city, the vice president worked on the planning committee and became responsible for arranging one of the tracks of presentations at the conference. He called on the company's manager of training for guidance in arranging for consultants to present the workshops involved, and the two worked as a team on the project. To show his gratitude, the vice president made sure that others knew how skilled and knowledgeable the manager was; and at a later date the vice president fought for increased funding for the training function.

8

Administering and Marketing Programs

The success of a program is related to how well it is planned and produced. Many small details need attention. Corners can be cut and certain amenities left out as cost-saving efforts, but good organization and thoroughness in planning add immeasurably to program outcome. Individuals who have trouble with all the jigsaw-puzzle pieces that make up the final product will find that relying on administrative support, automated equipment, and planning can make the entire effort feel less overwhelming and run more smoothly.

The most creatively designed and well-run program will fail if the audience is not interested in the content. Conscientious and thoughtful marketing of programs increases the likelihood of attendance by appropriate participants. The processes of administering and marketing programs are intricately intertwined.

PERSONNEL

It is very important to clarify the nature and extent of the administrative and secretarial support that is available and to determine which individuals can assist with the administrative work of program production. Clarifying the other responsibilities of those chosen can prevent potentially conflicting demands that might place the chosen helpers in an uncomfortable situation.

With thorough advance planning, heavy work periods often can be predicted and creative efforts made to use available support. Some personnel may be able to help periodically or in a crunch. If internal personnel are unavailable to help during high-volume work periods, there may be funds to hire temporary help. Planning can contribute significantly to the effective use of office temporaries. For example, a trainer may collect handouts that need to be typed and hire a typist for an afternoon; similarly, a trainer may arrange application deadlines for programs so that an office temporary with word-processing skills can enter all of the applicant data for several programs at one time.

Interns and volunteers can be an additional source of help. Sometimes students and others who are interested in investigating the field of training and development want some experience. Local colleges with communications programs might place interns to assist with projects. For example, an intern could help to produce video vignettes, write role-play scripts, or review and select handouts for programs. Student help is often quite inexpensive as well as flexible in availability. Because policies regarding the employment of students and the use of volunteers and interns differ, it is important to find out about precedents before investigating this option.

It is also important to give thought to the training and development of the support troops. Their education can be thought of as a microcosm of a training intervention. The trainer needs to find out what their career goals and plans are and then try to provide experiences that will contribute to these objectives. For example, an administrative assistant might be willing to teach keyboard skills during a program for managers who want to use interactive computers; in return the assistant would gain visibility and make connections that might lead to future job opportunities. In working with support people, it is a good idea to try to model behaviors that will add to their effectiveness; for example, the use of good time-management skills and thorough planning might encourage similar behaviors.

Support personnel can contribute enormously to the design and implementation of systems that deal with the details of program production. Such personnel should be encouraged to think creatively about how to streamline processes, cut paperwork, or do two things at once. Because these people are often experienced at organizing details, they can develop excellent systems and schemes for accomplishing this purpose.

MARKETING PROGRAMS

Some programs are designed in response to requests from specific departments or divisions and are geared toward a specific audience, while others encourage participation from a large segment of the organization. In either case, information must be provided about program goals, content, format, and registration procedures. Any contact with potential participants before a program begins is, in effect, a form of marketing. The more consistently these efforts are thought of as marketing, the higher is the likelihood that they will be effective. Whenever a new program or development opportunity is launched, thought should be given to formulating a marketing strategy. As Gafner (1986, p. 54) says, "People don't do things for your reasons, they do things for their reasons. . . . They've got to see what it will do for them, personally and professionally."

The trainer needs to think carefully about the individuals who will benefit most from a given program. The data generated during the needs-assessment process can be analyzed to determine appropriate participant populations. Then the trainer can formulate strategies that let potential participants know how they will benefit. In establishing and communicating benefits, it is important to be realistic but to sell the program so that the likelihood of its success is increased. Information about program goals and objectives can be provided so that people know what they can realistically expect to accomplish or learn by attending. Individuals who enroll by informed choice tend to be more cooperative and receptive than those who are not clear about the reason for their attendance.

Program titles can reflect true program content and appeal to the targeted audience; these titles influence the expectations of participants. Also, it is important to be consistent in designing marketing communications to allow for recognition and ease of understanding. Program booklets can be organized so that readers easily can find the necessary information about a program's content, its benefits, and the registration procedures. In some organizations it is a good idea to create and use a logo to designate the origin of all communications concerning training and development and to reproduce all communications on a single color of paper stock to encourage quick recognition.

Mailings cost money; decisions must be made about to whom to send them. At times it makes sense to include everyone in an organization. If, for instance, an increase in visibility of training programs is needed, or if there is a desire for all members of the organization to feel that they have equal access to programs, a general mailing may actually be the most cost-effective way to accomplish these goals. Other programs are designed or designated for specific segments of the population and require smaller, more specialized mailings.

Example: Designating target audiences.

The training department at a large research and design company offered a workshop entitled "Effective Writing Skills." The program was usually open to everyone who wrote during the course of their jobs. On one occasion, however, a decision was made to offer the program specifically to the engineers and scientists who had to write technical reports and journal articles about their work. Letters were sent to potential participants explaining the content and format of the program. Because there was concern that some individuals would choose not to attend because of their discomfort with being critiqued in front of others, positive quotes were included from previous participants specifically addressing this concern. The credentials of the presenter were enumerated as well as his previous work with similar populations of engineers and scientists.

Although the program that was open to the general company population had been running for several years, the mailings for this specific program generated responses from many individuals who had never attended training programs at the company. The effort to tailor the program to a segment of the total population and market it to that segment was extremely successful.

When letters or memos about a program are sent to a targeted population, information that explains the potential usefulness of the program can be included. This information needs to, as Katz (1984, p. 78) says, ". . . address the concerns and requirements of the participants." He goes on to say that participants can actually be hostile if they come to a program misinformed about its focus or relevance.

Sometimes program information is sent in a memo to supervisors and managers for general distribution to their staffs. This approach either can result in loss of visibility for the memo or can generate the names of those individuals who would be the most appropriate participants. Supervisors and managers may be asked to nominate people for a program or for a selection committee's review or to distribute a memo to generate volunteer applicants. Each of these choices has different implications. Programs with nomination and selection committees may be seen as more desirable or as elitist. Some senior personnel will not attend voluntary programs because they doubt the worth of those programs. It is essential to think about the audience sought for a specific program, to formulate a strategy that will increase the appeal of that program for the targeted group, and to ensure that the chosen strategy is consistent with general philosophy or policies about training and development in the company.

Marketing efforts can include many kinds of communication: fliers announcing an offering, longer mailings with specific information on programs, individually addressed letters describing the benefits to a particular person, or informational mailings like articles or newsletters that can be an intervention on their own.

Example: Expanding the influence of training efforts through mailings.

A manager of training and development had received a number of requests for help from newly promoted supervisors. A program for new supervisors was offered only twice a year, and those calling wanted assistance while they waited to attend the program. The training manager, with the help of other members of the personnel office, put together a packet of handouts for new supervisors. This packet included a copy of the personnel policy delineating the responsibilities of supervisors, some readings on effective supervision, a resource list of people available to supervisors, a list and schedule of workshops offered on skills of supervision, and a bibliography.

The training manager sent the packet to all supervisors with a letter explaining that in the future it would be sent to all new supervisors. She asked the existing supervisors to read the packets and make suggestions about what else might be included. As a result of this approach, the distributed materials were read by many supervisors who would never attend a program because their attendance might be taken to mean that they did not know their jobs. Later that year, near the time of annual performance reviews, she sent another packet on feedback and performance discussions to all supervisors. The letter accompanying this packet asked for the supervisors' help in reviewing the relevance of the articles enclosed.

The question of how often to send mailings also needs to be considered. Aside from obvious concerns about cost, there are also considerations regarding what is most effective. It is essential to find a balance between establishing training as a recognizable, accessible function and maintaining a cost- and time-conscious profile. A barrage of frequent, lengthy memos often remains unread.

Existing communication resources such as newsletters within the organization can be used; information about upcoming training efforts can be made newsworthy and then given to appropriate individuals. The trainer can establish relationships that can increase the visibility of the training function, for example, letting the editor of an internal newsletter know when an interesting training trend is evolving. It is possible to accomplish the goal of informing people about training events while respecting the limits of good taste and company norms.

Example: Creatively promoting a program.

A program that was established for employees in a university consisted of talks delivered by faculty members. These talks, which concerned the faculty members' research, were delivered in nonscientific language. Arrangements were made for a student, dressed as Darth Vader, to introduce a faculty member's talk on President Reagan's Star Wars initiative. The campus news office was informed of the event before it occurred, and the weekly paper included a photo and an article about the talk.

DEVELOPING SYSTEMS

It is advisable to use systems to keep track of the administrative details involved in running training programs and to collect and track data. Such systems can facilitate the best use of limited time. All repetitive tasks, ongoing tasks, and reports can be organized so that each time they are needed the methods to accomplish them are almost automatic. For example, the trainer might want to develop a simple system to keep track of films that are previewed; this system might include a way to note which films have been ordered or previewed, when they were previewed, and when they were returned. A list of questions to answer while viewing films might also be constructed. Information about a film's content and applicability is easy to compile while previewing the film but difficult to reconstruct later; a system for collecting this information limits the chance of reordering a film that was already seen, provides reviews to read when a film is needed for a new program, and allows development of future previewing plans.

It is also a good idea to devise a system to handle the organization and inventory of handouts used in programs. For example, the trainer would probably want to maintain lists of the handouts that are needed for each session of all programs that are regularly repeated; in this way quantities of needed handouts can be ordered or reproduced at the beginning of each training cycle if storage is available. The originals of such handouts can be kept in such a way that they can be located easily. It is very time consuming to create lists of potential handouts each time a program is repeated.

Reports that are written regularly are also candidates for being prepared according to a system. In devising such a system, the trainer might decide what types of data to collect for the reports, the purpose of the report, and its audience; find out the kinds of data that key individuals would be most interested in having; consider what kinds of data would help to sell the training effort; and investigate in what forms comparable data are available (for example, data from similar organizations that might be used in the report for comparison). Forethought about format and purpose can greatly decrease the time and effort involved in collection and can increase the usefulness of the data and the ease which which the data are used.

Many kinds of information can be collected and the collection process systematized. For example, systems can be developed to keep track of the number of participants and/or applicants per program, the number of participant hours per program or per presenter, or the cost per participant or program. By clarifying data needs, the trainer can streamline a system so that only needed and wanted data are collected.

Systems can be established to keep track of program participants. Lists of all participants during a year can be retained so that these people can be contacted for retrospective evaluations of programs. This kind of contact can have the added benefit of increasing participants' feelings of connection and involvement in the training effort.

The use of any and all available automation can be helpful in developing systems. For example, it is advisable to beg, borrow, or barter for the use of a word processor, personal computer, or electronic typewriter. It may be necessary to convince the person responsible for purchasing equipment for the training function that automation will greatly increase both the effectiveness and the extent of training programs; if so, it can be pointed out that a personal computer does not receive employee benefits and that it can keep and process information much more quickly and easily than an employee can by hand. Automated equipment can be used to maintain a data base and provide numbers or names for reports, studies, and planning purposes. The list-processing features of word processors and personal computers are time-saving ways to store data about participants as well as to generate correspondence to participants and their supervisors, attendance and participant lists, and mailing labels. Also, codes can be devised to identify specific populations from longer lists for targeted mailings (for example, all supervisors and managers).

Consistency in methods used for filing information, whether in a file cabinet or on a personal computer, will aid the retrieval process. The trainer needs to decide on a system that allows for the greatest ease in retrieval. For example, handouts can be filed by program or by topic; but regardless of the system chosen, they should be filed in such a way that originals can be found readily and an estimate of the number of copies on hand can be determined easily.

It is also important to devise a system for organizing the details of program registration. Depending on the nature of the information desired, registration can be accomplished by mail, by telephone, or in person at the event. The following questions about registration need to be answered:

- Will there be a registration deadline? How much time is needed between the deadline and the program?
- Will confirmations of acceptance into programs be sent to applicants?
- Will applicants' supervisors be notified of their participation in programs?
- What will happen if there is an overwhelming response to a program? Will the program be repeated so that all applicants can attend? How will choices be made about who can attend? How will those not able to attend be notified?

Systems can allow for consistency, thoughtfulness, and thoroughness. They should be created to accomplish the goals and objectives of the training function rather than to control the function in a rigid manner. Any training function must remain flexible and responsive while managing endless details, and well-designed systems can help in this process.

Check lists of details that need attention before, during, and after a program can decrease the likelihood of slip-ups and conserve time. Figure 6 is an example of a check list for an on-site training program. It can easily be modified to meet individual needs.

Program Planning

1. Decide who will plan program, membership, and responsibilities:
   - individuals
   - committee
   - advisory group
   - task group
2. Decide who will make decisions and what processes will be used for decision making:
   - administrative decisions
   - budgetary decisions
   - decisions on program content
3. Establish timelines of dates and deadlines:
   - marketing processes
   - application/registration process
   - content design
   - printed materials
   - evaluation procedures

Program Content

1. Clarify goals and objectives.
2. Gather information from potential participants, their supervisors, etc.
3. Research and choose content areas.
4. Choose and orient presenters.
5. Design program.
6. Choose and design handouts, prework, and follow-up readings.
7. Create bibliography.

**Figure 6. Example of a Check List
for an On-Site Training Program**

Program Finances

1. Determine program cost.
2. Secure or designate funding sources.
3. Develop systems to track funds received and spent.

Participants

1. Choose audience.
2. Develop strategy to attract participants and to market program.
3. Design application/registration procedures:
   - due dates
   - destination of forms
   - procedures to be used at actual event
4. Decide maximum/minimum number of participants.
5. Develop process to be used to select individual participants.
6. Produce printed materials:
   - memos
   - fliers
   - announcements
   - application/registration materials
   - letters of confirmation and/or rejection
   - communications to participants' supervisors
7. Produce or develop mailing lists and printed labels.

Scheduling

1. Choose date and time for program.
2. Schedule presenters.

**Figure 6 (continued). Example of a Check List
for an On-Site Training Program**

3. Determine details/requirements with presenters:
   - date
   - time
   - place
   - preferences for type of room
   - furniture in room
   - audiovisual needs
   - dates and times of planning meetings
   - fees
   - number of participants
4. Schedule room.
5. Arrange for:
   - key to room
   - setup and cleanup of room
   - audiovisual equipment and operators
   - refreshments
   - parking for presenters and/or participants
   - ventilation
   - supplies: newsprint, felt-tipped markers, masking tape, easels
6. Determine schedule for printed materials.

Preparations for the Event

1. Have ready:
   - name tags
   - attendance list
   - list of participants
   - handouts, notebooks, pencils, and paper

**Figure 6 (continued). Example of a Check List
for an On-Site Training Progam**

2. Prepare for evaluation process:
   - Design and print forms.
   - Decide on distribution and retrieval systems.
   - Design tabulation and analysis processes.
   - Decide what to do with results.
   - Design reports and decide on recipients.
3. Check audiovisual equipment.
4. Make arrangements for dismantling equipment, rearranging room as necessary, etc., after event.
5. Decide how to/who will convene session.
6. Decide how to/who will end session.

After the Program

1. Summarize, tabulate, analyze evaluations.
2. Distribute evaluation information.
3. File copies of all materials.
4. Make notes for improving processes, procedures, content, etc.
5. Write letters of appreciation and send payments to presenters.
6. Write letters and/or send follow-up materials to participants.

**Figure 6 (continued). Example of a Check List
for an On-Site Training Program**

SCHEDULING

Organizations run on cycles or schedules. Thought should be given to the natural cycle that occurs within the company:

- Are activities based on a fiscal, an academic, or a chronological year?
- Are there slower times when people might be more willing to attend time-consuming training programs?
- Are there busy times when short, focused programs on working under stress would be well attended?

It is important to use knowledge of the organizational cycle to plan the program cycle. Slow times can be used to plan and design new programs, evaluate past efforts, develop new systems, and write reports.

Scheduling involves keeping track of many details. Sessions must be scheduled, including rooms and presenters. Time must be allowed for setting up and dismantling equipment and for rearranging furniture. Decisions about when to schedule a program should take into consideration the needs of the target population. For example, to allow different shifts of employees the opportunity to attend certain programs, the trainer might consider scheduling individual sessions at different times and on different days. Before scheduling programs, it is essential to check carefully for dates of holidays, religious observances, celebrations, or local school vacation weeks when many parents take their vacations.

The timetable for a program actually goes from Z to A to Z. Once the date for a program has been set, therefore, the trainer should work backward from that date to schedule the first steps. An extra-large one- or two-month calendar can make this task easier. It can be quite calming to see a complete schedule set forth in black and white and to feel totally in control.

COST CONCERNS

The training and development function is budgeted differently from organization to organization. Sometimes the training function falls within the personnel budget; sometimes it has its own budget; and sometimes it needs to produce enough income to be at least partially self-supporting. The costs of staff salaries and benefits are sometimes funded differently from consultant fees and operating expenses. Whatever method is used to fund programs, there needs to be agreement about who is reponsible for which expenditures, who has the power to approve or veto expenditures, and in which circumstances approval is necessary prior to making a financial commitment.

Once the responsibility and authority for a budget are clear, administrative decisions can be made with budgetary limitations in mind. For instance, options for the production of handouts and brochures can range from typeset, custom-designed versions to photocopied, word-processed copy. Programs can include lavish buffet meals, only coffee, or no provisions for meals or coffee breaks.

Amenities such as meals can add status to programs and may be worth the monetary investment. People and issues to consider in determining how to use funds include the audience, the climate in the organization concerning visible use of funds, organizational norms, the desired impact, and other demands on budget dollars.

Sometimes what seems like a conscious effort to cut costs and stay within a designated budget can result in higher costs than originally planned. For example, the money-saving effort of using unpaid or low-cost temporary labor must be balanced against the time investment to train and supervise this staff.

The trainer should try to be as creative as possible in achieving goals and conserving available funds. Barter is one effective method for obtaining services.

Example: Trading services to lower program costs.

A director of training at a university was hired with the agreement that she had to make her function self-supporting within one year. She had to recover operating costs, not salaries or benefits. Three months into her job she realized that one of her largest costs was for coffee and donuts. She did not want to exclude refreshments entirely, although she began to cut back on this expense. She noticed that many of the university's food-service employees were attending the programs that she offered. She approached the manager of food services and asked him to consider a trade of catering for her programs in exchange for tailored, on-site training programs for his employees. A very favorable arrangement was worked out. Not only did she reduce the considerable costs of program catering, but she also began to realize one of her goals: establishing a reputation for conducting tailored, in-house training programs.

POLITICAL IMPLICATIONS

Many administrative and marketing decisions have both obvious and subtle political implications. It is important to think through possible outcomes and repercussions before implementing a new marketing strategy or administrative system. Decisions can then be made with open eyes, and they can be backed by plans that will increase the likelihood of success.

Decisions about the visibility of the training function often have wider repercussions than planned. Marketing involves efforts to generate visibility for programs and, consequently, for the training function as a whole. Marketing efforts can cause the community to view training as linked to certain segments of the population. For example, a large-scale effort with lots of public fanfare launching a support-staff training effort may cause those client groups interested in management training to doubt the ability of the internal staff to provide training relevant to their needs. It is essential to keep a balanced public profile in order to have an impact on a cross section of the organization.

Decisions involving cost concerns often have widespread significance. Some managers of training functions push hard to have control over independent budgets. While this strategy may be best in some organizations where functions are not taken seriously without budgetary responsibility, in other organizations this could be a real mistake. Some small training functions have survived widespread organizational budget cuts because they were hidden within a general, personnel/human resource department budget.

Decisions about communications with the organizational population are influenced by cost concerns in less-obvious ways. In some companies it is most important to maximize the impact of communications while minimizing the amount of money that is spent on communication materials. Sometimes it is more important that a booklet of program descriptions look and be low cost, and less important that it be graphically attractive. Senior management might be especially concerned with cost containment and might prefer a plain product produced from simple, word-processed copy instead of a slick, award-winning design. On the other hand, it might be worthwhile to produce beautifully illustrated and designed products for a senior managers' conference to add status to the offering. Both short-term and long-term goals should be considered when planning marketing and administrative strategies; what will be most successful and best supported in the organization should be assessed.

Little details of program administration can have amazing repercussions. For example, copies of letters sent to program applicants confirming their participation can be sent to their supervisors as well. This approach can increase supervisors' awareness of who is taking advantage of the programs, the scope of the programs being offered, and the need for office coverage as a result of employees' participation in programs. Some participants want their supervisors to know of their efforts to learn new skills and become more effective, while other employees may react adversely to their supervisors' receiving copies of notification letters and perceive the process as a way to check on their whereabouts.

Letters, memos, fliers, and booklets announcing programs may originate from the training department or elsewhere, depending on the market for a particular offering. For example, a program for supervisors might have a larger subscription if a letter is sent from the vice president in charge of the area than if it originates from the training office. Endorsements from senior management should be used wisely and conservatively to preserve their impact.

Devoting time and attention to political implications can reap valuable dividends. Careful planning and forethought can prevent problems and ensure consistency in program quality and effectiveness.

9

Developing As a Professional

Even though trainers spend their lives helping others to deal with job-related stress and burnout, all too often they resemble the cobbler's children with holes in their shoes. As professionals, they need to take the same care and time in planning their own development and renewal as they do in planning programs; just as they are guided by desires to help participants to feel empowered at work and at home, they need to be guided by the same desires for themselves. Trainers need to feel supported and nurtured in order to be on stage in training programs, truly receptive to participants, creative in designing programs, well organized, and enthusiastic. Managing stress and preventing burnout are difficult tasks that demand creative and individualized solutions. Consequently, trainers must be conscientiously self-aware about their individual renewal and growth needs, and they must be proactive in meeting those needs.

DEVELOPING COLLEGIAL RELATIONSHIPS

The need for awareness of development and renewal is heightened for individuals who work alone or in small training functions. The fact that many trainers have few internal colleagues increases the importance of meeting and interacting with other trainers outside the home organization.

Close relationships with colleagues provide many benefits and are validating for trainers who usually work alone. Contact with colleagues combats the voice-in-the-wilderness feeling experienced by solitary professionals. It provides a yardstick by which to measure strengths, weaknesses, successes, and failures. Professionals can develop a clearer sense of themselves, where they excel, and how they need to grow by comparing themselves with other professionals. Such comparisons provide the trainer with role models, mentors, colleagues, and students. It is much easier to have a vision of a future as a professional after exposure to many professional options, and becoming acquainted with colleagues and their organizations can help in this process.

Developing and maintaining relationships with colleagues can also help in the prevention and management of stress. Feeling validated, recognizing successes, being realistic about limits and weaknesses, and identifying oneself as a member of a profession all contribute to self-esteem and satisfaction.

Finding out what other trainers have been able to do and what they have not accomplished creates a context for assessing work demands. Most trainers can dream up enough work to keep a team busy for years. It is sometimes hard to be realistic about what can actually be accomplished. Discussing involvements and accomplishments with others provides a more reasonable limit to efforts. Then the crucial step becomes choosing the right tasks to do as opposed to trying to do everything.

One important function of a collegial relationship is to provide a receptive port in a storm. During difficult times it is good to have another knowledgeable professional to talk to, complain to, strategize with, and receive support from—all in confidence.

Also, colleagues can help one another to avoid reinventing the wheel each time a new program is planned. Rarely are genuinely new ideas produced in this world. Meeting others who have dealt with similar problems, designed similar programs, or trained similar participants can prevent the replication of mistakes and allow for improvement on previous efforts. Many trainers are very willing to share their efforts with colleagues. This approach is consistent with the values that they are preaching, and they can benefit from reciprocation.

It is important to realize, though, that some trainers are very guarded about program designs. Sometimes they do not want to share because they think they have created marketable products. In reality, a design is only what a trainer is able to do with it. A skillful trainer will be hired for that skill, not for the program design alone. In addition, many designs are generic and have wide application. Nevertheless, it is essential to acknowledge the origin of shared ideas and to ask permission to use them; another's ideas should never be used as if they were one's own.

CULTIVATING SUPPORT WITHIN THE ORGANIZATION

Debates in the literature on the relative importance of support from top management usually concentrate on its impact on allocation of resources, choices of projects, and outcomes of training. A less obvious, but extremely important, result of support within an organization—from top management, line management, and the grass roots—is the impact on trainers. In environments in which trainers are often struggling for survival, life can be very stressful; support, with its validating and nourishing effects, is essential. With support, individuals can produce abundantly with limited resources and yet experience little resulting stress. Trainers need to cultivate internal support at all levels, not only for the sake of survival but also to prevent stress and promote job satisfaction.

DEVELOPING SKILLS AND ABILITIES

Training and development professionals perform many roles. They use a variety of skills and abilities, depending on their roles at any given time. Some of these skills and abilities are tied to the role of trainer in a workshop; some are required by administrative responsibilities; some are important when working as a consultant; some are crucial to marketing and sales efforts; and some are needed in the role of counselor. It is important for trainers to think about their individual jobs and to develop skills that not only support these functions but also promote their own career development.

In the past few years, much has been written on the skills and abilities that are needed to be an effective trainer. These studies and articles yield information that can guide quests for professional development. For example, the report of the American Society for Training and Development (ASTD) Competency Study, *Models for Excellence* (McLagan, 1983), delineates a framework for the skills required in the field of training and development. The study proposes fifteen key roles performed by training and development professionals: evaluator, group facilitator, individual development counselor, instructional writer, instructor, manager of training and development, marketer, media specialist, needs analyst, program administrator, program designer, strategist, task analyst, theoretician, and transfer agent. This list was devised through reviews of the literature and as a result of surveys and questionnaires administered to experts in the training and development field. Although not all trainers are expected to fill all of these roles, all trainers do need to perfect the skills that are inherent in the roles they are required to perform.

Also identified in the literature are the characteristics that are central to success in many of these roles. Writers have pinpointed some of these characteristics by studying expert or master trainers. Four of the central themes that emerge in various accounts of these characteristics are extensive self-awareness, infectious enthusiasm, expertise as a facilitator of learning, and excellence as a listener.

Increasing Self-Awareness

Underlying an individual's efforts to become an expert trainer is a need to integrate personal and professional growth. To be effective in the field of training, professionals must be willing to re-examine themselves, frequently and critically, and to try to improve continually. The best trainers are people who are self-confident because they know and can admit that they have limits and weaknesses.

Sometimes new trainers are not very self-confident, and this lack of self-confidence can be revealed in many different ways. Others who have been in the field a while lose their perspective about their own strengths and weaknesses and act as if they believe they are better or wiser than the participants in a workshop. However, trainers are more effective when they are honest with themselves and with others about their strengths, their limitations, and their concerns. This does not mean, for example, that new trainers must go on ad nauseum about their inexperience and cause participants to be skeptical about their abilities; but all trainers do need to admit when they do not know something. Groups of participants can have expertise that a trainer does not have, and validating that knowledge and using it as a complement to the trainer's own expertise can create an exciting learning experience.

Periodic involvement in situations that provide self-assessment, feedback, and demonstration of skills can be useful in maintaining a realistic notion of one's strengths and weaknesses. In other words, a trainer needs to practice what he or she preaches: the integration of personal growth and awareness with professional growth and awareness.

Maintaining Enthusiasm

An enthusiastic trainer can create an environment of excitement, energy, and acceptance. As Lynton and Pareek (1967) say:

> The kinds of feeling that matter for a favorable climate include an absorbing interest and feeling of excitement in his subject and his work of training; eagerness to share the task and help participants grow into taking more responsibility for it; acceptance of the participants as people with differing needs and personalities, and responsiveness to them; and trust in himself and in others. (p. 278)

It is impossible for trainers to communicate enthusiasm if they are feeling burned out or under so much pressure that they cannot give their full attention to the tasks at hand. Taking care of themselves as individuals and professionals provides the kind of renewal needed for continued enthusiasm.

Facilitating Learning

There is a world of difference between teaching a subject and facilitating learning. Trainers need to see themselves realistically and not as people who know everything and are going to give their knowledge to others. Laird and Belcher (1984) write about the importance of having and expressing belief in students' ability to achieve and allowing students to learn in different ways. Professionals who see themselves as facilitators "nourish individual differences" (Laird & Belcher, p. 73) in how people learn as opposed to trying to force knowledge on participants. Good facilitators are comfortable with the fact that people learn in a variety of ways, and they strive to create environments that encourage all types of learning. Trainers need to be secure in the knowledge that people will learn in their own ways and that trainers are just instruments or catalysts in the process.

Trainers should use many methods to address the wide variety of individual learning styles. They also should be willing to make use of all events that happen for the purpose of learning. As Laird and Belcher (1984, p.75) write, "Who can say that unplanned learning is less useful than what was originally intended?" This attitude requires flexibility and self-confidence; professionals who are committed to completing a planned design often are unaware of spontaneous opportunities for learning.

Becoming an Excellent Listener

In many of the roles required of training and development professionals, listening is a major activity. Trainers need to model true commitment to building, maintaining, and using effective listening skills. To sharpen their own listening abilities, they can participate in workshops, seek feedback from colleagues and workshop participants, use training materials, view videotapes of their presentations with willing participants, and watch experts on active listening in action. Effective listening does not just happen; professionals need to work at it continually.

CHOOSING WORK

Trainers need to use the same skills of time management, planning, goal clarification, delegation, stress management, and energy conservation that they encourage others to use. Doing so will not only help them to plan their efforts and to feel less stressed, but also will help them to relate to the problems that participants experience with these issues.

Although some responsibilities are dictated by, or at least highly influenced by, other people, one does have choices about how to invest energy and time. Periodically it is enlightening for trainers to re-examine the criteria that they have been using to make choices about their work. For example, a trainer may choose a project for any of the following reasons:

- The boss requests it.
- A similar project has already been completed; therefore, the new project will take very little time.

- The project involves a topic that the trainer is interested in learning more about.
- It would be interesting to work with the people involved.
- The project has high visibility.
- It makes practical sense to become involved in the project.

Whatever criteria are used, the resulting nature of the work needs to be examined. From the standpoint of stress management and professional development, it is important that a balance is found between choosing projects that offer challenge and growth and saying "no" to projects that lead nowhere, deplete resources, and are not central to either personal or organizational goals. In reality, individuals become involved in some activities because of organizational politics; but often there is room for choice.

New trainers tend to find everything challenging and anxiety producing. As the newness wears off, they need to choose projects that continue to generate excitement and growth. All trainers need to pay attention to which projects they are drawn toward and which ones they consistently avoid. Trainers need to examine and confront their own resistances. By doing so they reap an additional benefit by becoming more effective in dealing with resistance in participants. Trainers may also find that talking with their supervisors or colleagues can help in understanding these issues.

An opportunity to supervise or manage others can be challenging and can increase a trainer's effectiveness with program participants. Trainers who have never tried to use the skills they teach are limited by their imagination. Giving constructive feedback to someone who is being arrogant or difficult is very different from discussing a case in a workshop for supervisors. At some point in a trainer's career, it can be quite useful to gain this type of direct experience and thereby begin to close the credibility gap.

Making more conscious and thoughtful decisions about which projects to be involved in, which projects to reject, and which new endeavors to attempt can add variety and excitement to the job and reduce stress.

SEEKING FORMAL EVALUATION AND FEEDBACK

The professional associations for training and development have been studying and proposing various schema for certification and review as another avenue for professional development. Although none of these proposed schema has as yet been widely endorsed, all professional trainers are encouraged to seek feedback and evaluation within their companies and from colleagues.

One method of establishing a formal procedure of evaluation involves peer review. Trainers who belong to local or regional associations or are members of informal professional groups (for example, trainers in the insurance industry or women trainers) can attempt to establish a peer review process. Such a process might involve a formal check list and a schedule of rotation of review assignments; or it might consist of a more informal agreement that several peers will visit, assess, and provide feedback on the training function in another organization. An agreement needs to be reached initially on the goals, objectives, areas of review, and nature of feedback desired. This process can be a valuable experience for a trainer who works alone in an organization; has no internal colleagues with professional expertise in training; and has limited opportunities to receive specific, comparative feedback. Although the idea of engaging in peer reviews can be quite frightening, the use of effective diagnosis, feedback, and listening skills can provide help in evaluation and planning.

Rothwell (1985, p. 78) points out, "Peer review is at once a time to shine professionally and to gain fresh insights from colleagues who may have experienced similar problems." He goes on to say that peer review can cause top management to focus on the training department, that ". . . the opinions of outside experts may carry weight with senior management, and outside experts can identify achievements as well as deficiencies in the products of the department, or in adverse conditions under which the department is forced to function." Peer reviews can provide benefits to the organization being reviewed in terms of feedback and helpful visibility.

STRATEGIES FOR DEVELOPMENT

In a discussion of *Careers in Training and Development* (Hutcheson & Otte, 1981) published by ASTD, the authors of that paper remark:

> Trainers go through various career stages, and different roles or functions become important as they progress. Persons often want to look good as presenters; later they want to show mastery of the field they teach. They may be more concerned with the content

to be taught, organizing it, developing and using audio-visual materials, determining appropriate approaches to training, stating clear objectives and producing well-designed programs. Still later, they may shift their focus from being a presenter and expert to being an organizational problem-solver. At this stage they may want to enlarge their organizational development, consulting, and counseling roles. Toward the end of a career in training, the focus may be upon sharing with others in the training field, creating new ways of doing things, and organizing what is known about the field for teaching it to others. (p. 2)

Individuals need to adopt strategies for development that address their career goals and then progress through these stages.

The paragraphs that follow offer specific ideas for accomplishing some of the development tasks discussed earlier in this chapter:

1. *Make contact with trainers in other organizations.* Join a formal professional organization. Most include regional and national groups that have regular meetings and periodic workshops and conferences. Examples are as follows:

- American Society for Training and Development (ASTD)
  1630 Duke Street, Box 1443
  Alexandria, VA 22313
  (703) 683-8100
- National Society for Performance and Instruction (NSPI)
  1126 16th Street, N.W., Suite 214
  Washington, DC 20036
  (202) 861-0777
- Organization Development Network (ODN)
  1011 Park Avenue
  Plainfield, NJ 07060
  (201) 561-8677

Less-formal professional associations also exist. For example, those responsible for training the staffs of colleges and universities in the Boston area meet yearly to discuss the issues that they encounter and to share their successes and failures. Members of the group also contact one another during the year to share information on programs and designs.

Support groups of trainers in a particular field or specialty can also be formed. For example, over the course of several years, a group of women trainers met monthly to share their experiences; this group existed as long as its members felt that it served a useful purpose for them.

2. ***Plan work in such a way that burnout is prevented and personal energy is increased.*** Determine a cycle for the program year. Depending on the work setting, programs are based on a fiscal, a chronological, a seasonal, or an academic year. Determining a cycle encourages recognition of the busiest times and the slowest times and allows better use of slow times for rejuvenation and growth. Knowing that there is a light at the end of a long tunnel can help in maintaining energy through stressful times.

At the end of each cycle, review accomplishments. Make decisions about programs for the next cycle based on observations of the data. Discontinue or postpone programs if fewer participants are interested or trainer enthusiasm is ebbing. Create new programs to keep interest and investment. Think about career progression, professional development, and job satisfaction. Use career-development instruments or create some other structure that helps in the completion of a review process. Using a format such as the one shown in Figure 7 is one way to begin to assess career development and to plan actions for the next year.

PROFESSIONAL-DEVELOPMENT REVIEW SHEET

1. Jot down answers to the following questions:
   - When you think about your growth as a professional, which people, experiences, workshops, books, and so forth stand out as significant contributors to your development?
   - When you think about your growth as a professional *during this past year,* which people, experiences, workshops, books, and so forth stand out as significant contributors to your development?

2. Analyze your answers:
   - What trends appeared in your answers?
   - What direction do you want to take in the next year?
   - Which contributors yielded the biggest payoff? Do you want more of these contributors?
   - What was missing from your list that might have been a significant contributor?

Figure 7. Example of a Professional-Development Review Sheet

3. ***Attend professional workshops and conferences.***
Trainers have a reputation for believing in lifelong learning, and that belief should apply to themselves as well as to trainees. Choose workshops and conferences by comparing their content with training-program requirements during the next cycle or during the next several years.

Choose opportunities that will allow observation of experts in action. Attend workshops presented by professionals with good reputations in order to experience their training styles. Observe how they handle situations that cause difficulty for you. Notice how they increase participation and what questions they ask. Not only will these experiences increase your repertoire of behaviors, but also they will allow you to measure yourself against some ideals.

Ask colleagues which conferences or workshops they have found to be the most useful. Carefully read brochures and catalogs, check references, and call the organization sponsoring the event or the actual presenter to ask questions or voice concerns.

Use the time at workshops and conferences to make contact with other participants. Socializing at these events can yield excellent resources for the future.

Attending workshops and conferences can rekindle flagging enthusiasm and provide a needed change of scene. Use the time to revel in the joy of being with peers and colleagues, to gain insights, and to gather new ideas to take back to the work site. Yearly conference information and schedules of workshops are available from the following sources:

- American Society for Training and Development (ASTD)
  1630 Duke Street
  Alexandria, VA 22313
- National Training Laboratories (NTL)
  1501 Wilson Boulevard
  Arlington, VA 22209
- Organization Development Network (ODN)
  1011 Park Avenue
  Plainfield, NJ 07060
- Lakewood Conferences
  50 South Ninth Street
  Minneapolis, MN 55402
- University Associates (UA)
  8517 Production Avenue
  San Diego, CA 92121

4. ***Use expositions and book displays at conferences to gain exposure to resources and ideas.*** Conference expositions provide a terrific opportunity to gather information in an efficient manner.

To get the most out of a conference exposition, think in advance about your needs for the next year or so. Decide which new programs will be presented or coordinated and which existing programs will be revamped. This process will help to clarify a focus for venturing into the exposition. Pick two or three areas of content or types of resources to explore. Examine the booklet of resources appearing at the exposition, and note which resources may fit identified needs. The first time you attend the exposition, talk only to those representatives whose resources you have selected. Bring a prepared list of questions and concerns, and explain the situation and your needs. Make notes, gather materials from these representatives, and exchange business cards with them. After talking to these people, attend the exposition again; this time cruise the aisles, enjoy the sights, taste the free popcorn, and find out about whatever seems interesting at the moment. This kind of planning will ensure leaving an exposition with usable information and contacts.

5. ***Attend workshops as a participant.*** For continuing personal growth and to learn new skills, attend some workshops as a participant. Attend a program that you sponsor to gain skills and to experience what it is like to be a participant. Also attend programs sponsored by external groups for exposure to other styles of training, to meet other professionals, and for additional personal growth.

6. ***Arrange opportunities to train and design programs with other trainers.*** This is particularly important if you usually work alone. Observing others' styles, receiving feedback from other professionals, and having the opportunity to debrief at the end of a session are experiences that lead to different perspectives. Working with other trainers can shake complacency, increase awareness of rigidity, and rekindle growth and change.

7. ***Write articles for publication and make presentations at conferences.*** At times it becomes important to consolidate ideas and experiences into a form that allows their communication to other professionals. Although exposing oneself in this way can be terrifying, it also affords opportunities for further growth, critical feedback, and contacts. Readers and listeners will challenge your

ideas, beliefs, and self-confidence; they will also validate your observations, experiences, and self-concept. All of this will encourage growth and development.

The field of training and development is exciting and growing. To be effective as professionals, trainers must keep their own excitement alive and encourage their own growth.

References and Bibliography

Abella, K.T. (1986). *Building successful training programs: A step-by-step guide.* Reading, MA: Addison-Wesley.

Andrews, E.S., & Noel, J.L. (1986). Adding life to the case-study method. *Training and Development Journal, 40,* 28-29.

Bell, C. (1984). Building a reputation for training effectiveness. *Training and Development Journal, 38,* 50-54.

Berdie, D.R., & Anderson, J.F. (1974). *Questionnaires: Design and use.* Metuchen, NJ: Scarecrow Press.

Boyd, B.B. (undated). Developing case studies: A six-step method for writing cases to fit special needs. In B.B. Boyd (Ed.), *Supervisory training: Approaches and methods* (pp. 99-108). Alexandria, VA: American Society for Training and Development.

Brinkerhoff, R.O. (1986). Expanding needs analysis. *Training and Development Journal, 40,* 64-65.

Caffarella, R. (1985). A checklist for planning successful training programs. *Training and Development Journal, 39,* 81-83.

Carnevale, A.P. (1986). The learning enterprise. *Training and Development Journal, 40,* 18-26.

Christensen, D.R., & Kinlaw, D.C. (1984). Management training: Managers can do it all—or almost all. *Training and Development Journal, 38,* 87-89.

Condon, M. (Ed.). (1985). Four by four: How do you start a training/HRD department from scratch? *Training and Development Journal, 39,* 12-20.

Craig, R.L. (Ed.). (1976). *Training and development: A guide to human resource development.* New York: McGraw-Hill.

Cureton, J.H., Newton, A.F., & Tesolowski, D.G. (1986). Finding out what managers need. *Training and Development Journal, 40*, 106-107.

Del Gaizo, E. (1984). Proof that supervisory training works! *Training and Development Journal, 38*, 30-31.

Desatnick, R.L. (1984). What makes the human resource function successful? *Training and Development Journal, 38*, 40-46.

Faris, J.P. (1984). How to use films in training. *Training and Development Journal, 38*, 108-110.

Fetteroll, E.C., Jr. (1985). 16 steps to increase your effectiveness. *Training and Development Journal, 39*, 68-70.

Gafner, R. (1986). Selling HRD on the inside. *Training and Development Journal, 40*, 54-56.

Gall, A.L. (Ed.). (1986). Four by four: How do you develop a training program on an unfamiliar topic? *Training and Development Journal, 40*, 22-25.

Georgenson, D., & Del Gaizo, E. (1984). Maximizing the return on your training investment through needs analysis. *Training and Development Journal, 38*, 42-47.

Germany, P.J., & Von Bergen, C.W., Jr. (1980, November). How to determine the training needs of your supervisors—when they're spread across the map. *Training: The Magazine of Human Resources Development*, pp. 55-56.

Gordon, J. (1986, June). What they don't teach you about being a training manager. *Training: The Magazine of Human Resources Development*, pp. 22-34.

Hutcheson, P., & Otte, F. (1981). *Careers in training and development*. Alexandria, VA: American Society for Training and Development.

Kaman, V.S. (1986). Why assessment interviews are worth it. *Training and Development Journal, 40*, 108-110.

Katz, T. (1984). Hostile audience, proceed with caution! *Training and Development Journal, 38*, 78-83.

Kelley, A.I., Orgel, R.F., & Baer, D.M. (1984). Evaluation: The bottom line is closer than you think. *Training and Development Journal, 38*, 32-37.

Kelley, A.I., Orgel, R.F., & Baer, D.M. (1985). Seven strategies that guarantee training transfer. *Training and Development Journal, 39,* 78-82.

Kirkpatrick, D.L. (1979). Techniques for evaluating training programs. *Training and Development Journal, 33,* 78-92.

Komras, H. (1985). Evaluating your training programs. *Training and Development Journal, 39,* 87-88.

Laird, D., & Belcher, F. (1984). How master trainers get that way. *Training and Development Journal, 38,* 73-75.

Lampe, S. (1986, October). Getting the most out of needs assessments. *Training: The Magazine of Human Resources Development,* pp. 101-104.

Lynton, R.P., & Pareek, U. (1967). *Training for development.* Homewood, IL: Richard D. Irwin.

Marx, R.D. (1986). Self managed skill retention. *Training and Development Journal, 40,* 54-57.

McLagan, P.A. (1983). *Models for excellence: The conclusions and recommendations of the ASTD training and development competency study.* Alexandria, VA: American Society for Training and Development.

Merwin, S. (1981). *Effective evaluation strategies and techniques: A key to successful training.* San Diego, CA: University Associates.

Michalak, D.F., & Yager, E.G. (1979). *Making the training process work.* New York: Harper & Row.

Nadler, L. (1976a). Improving the results of workshops, part I: Planning workshops. *Training and Development Journal, 30,* 3-8.

Nadler, L. (1976b). Improving the results of workshops, part II: Conducting workshops. *Training and Development Journal, 30,* 36-44.

Nadler, L. (1976c). Improving the results of workshops, part III: Linkage, evaluation and follow-up. *Training and Development Journal, 30,* 31-35.

Newstrom, J.W. (1975). Selecting training methodologies: A contingency approach. *Training and Development Journal, 29,* 12-16.

Pfeiffer, J.W. (1985). *Reference guide to handbooks and annuals.* San Diego, CA: University Associates.

Pfeiffer, J.W., & Jones, J.E. (Eds.). (1969). *A handbook of structured experiences for human relations training* (Vol. I). San Diego, CA: University Associates.

Quinn, S.R., & Karp, S. (1986). Developing an objective evaluation tool. *Training and Development Journal, 40,* 90-92.

Robinson, A.D. (1985). How to have a safe trip to the cutting edge. *Training and Development Journal, 39,* 45-48.

Robinson, D.G., & Robinson, J.C. (1985). Breaking barriers to skill transfer. *Training and Development Journal, 39,* 82-83.

Rothwell, W.J. (1985). The case for external peer review. *Training and Development Journal, 39,* 78-79.

Schein, E.H. (1969). *Process consultation: Its role in organization development.* Reading, MA: Addison-Wesley.

Scherer, J.J. (1984). How people learn: Assumptions for design. *Training and Development Journal, 38,* 64-65.

Schindler-Rainman, E., & Lippitt, R. (1975). *Taking your meetings out of the doldrums.* San Diego, CA: University Associates.

Schleger, P.R. (1984). What me produce video? *Training and Development Journal, 38,* 40-49.

Schlein, R.S., & Edgerton, N.M. (1985). Training: How to get it out of the classroom. *Training and Development Journal, 39,* 84-85.

Spitzer, D. (1979, May). Remember these dos and don'ts of questionnaire design. *Training: The Magazine of Human Resources Development,* pp. 34-37.

Stone, B.N. (1984). Looking back at a training design that failed. *Training and Development Journal, 38,* 63-66.

Stovall, R.G. (1975). Four steps to better training results: Improving training investment return. *Training and Development Journal, 29,* 18-19.

Swierczek, F.W., & Carmichael, L. (1985). The quantity and quality of evaluating training. *Training and Development Journal, 39,* 95-99.

Tracey, W.R. (1984). *Designing training and development systems.* New York: American Management Association.

Trapnell, G. (1984). Putting the evaluation puzzle together. *Training and Development Journal, 38,* 90-93.

Trost, A. (1985). They may love it but will they use it? *Training and Development Journal, 39,* 78-81.

Tyson, L.A., & Birnbauer, H. (1985). High-quality evaluation. *Training and Development Journal, 39,* 33-37.

Versaci, A.C. (1986). How's the business? *Training and Development Journal, 40,* 68-71.

Wlodkowski, R. (1985). Stimulation. *Training and Development Journal, 39,* 38-43.

Zemke, R. (1977, December). Task analysis: Figuring out what people need to learn. *Training: The Magazine of Human Resources Development,* pp. 16-20.

Zemke, R. (1978, December). How market research techniques can pay off for trainers. *Training: The Magazine of Human Resources Development,* pp. 48-49.

Zemke, R. (1979, April). Still trying to figure things out? Try using the critical incident method of analysis. *Training: The Magazine of Human Resources Development,* pp. 68-70.

Zemke, R., & Walonick, D. (1980, September). The non-statistician's approach to conducting and analyzing surveys. *Training: The Magazine of Human Resources Development,* pp. 89-96.

Zenger, J.H., & Hargis, K. (1982). Assessing training results: It's time to take the plunge! *Training and Development Journal, 36,* 10-16.